FAMINE AND COMMUNITY IN MULLINGAR POOR LAW UNION, 1845–1849

Mud Cabins and Fat Bullocks

Maynooth Studies in Local History

GENERAL EDITOR Raymond Gillespie

This pamphlet is one of eight new additions to the Maynooth Studies in Local History series in 1999. Like their twenty predecessors, most are based on theses submitted for the M.A. in Local History at National University of Ireland, Maynooth. The pamphlets are not concerned primarily with the portrayal of the history of 'particular places'. All are local in their focus but that localisation is determined not by administrative boundaries but rather the limits of the experience of everyday life in the regions of Ireland over time. In some of these works the local experience is of a single individual while in others social, occupational or religious groups form the primary focus of enquiry.

The results of these enquiries into the shaping of local societies in the past emphasises, again, the diversity of the Irish historical experience. Ranging across problems of economic disaster, political transformation, rural unrest and religious tension, these works show how such problems were grounded in the realities of everyday life in local communities. The responses to such challenges varied from region to region, each place coping with problems in its own way, determined by its historical evolution and contemporary constraints.

The result of such investigations can only increase our awareness of the complexity of Ireland's historical evolution. Each work, in its own right, is also a significant contribution to our understanding of how specific Irish communities have developed in all their richness and diversity. In all, they demonstrate the vibrancy and challenging nature of local history.

Maynooth Studies in Local History: Number 21

Famine and Community in Mullingar Poor Law Union, 1845–1849

Mud Cabins and Fat Bullocks

Seamus O'Brien

To Kathleen.
With best wishes
Seamus
Sept-8th
1999.

IRISH ACADEMIC PRESS
DUBLIN • PORTLAND, OR

First published in 1999 by
IRISH ACADEMIC PRESS
44, Northumberland Road, Dublin 4, Ireland
and in the United States of America by
IRISH ACADEMIC PRESS
c/o ISBS, 5804 NE Hassalo Street, Portland, OR 97213.

website: www.iap.ie

British Library Cataloguing in Publication Data
O'Brien, Seamus.
Famine and Community in Mullingar Poor Law Union, 1845–1849: Mud Huts and Fat Bullocks – (Maynooth studies in local history; 21)
1. Ireland – History – Famine, 1845–1852 2. Mullingar (Ireland) – Social conditions
I. Title
941.8 15 081

ISBN 0716526786

Library of Congress Cataloging-in-Publication Data
O'Brien, Seamus.
Famine and Community in Mullingar Poor Law Union, 1845–1849. Mud Huts and Fat Bullocks/Seamus O'Brien.
p. cm. — (Maynooth studies in local history: no. 21)
Includes bibliographical references and index.
ISBN 0–7165–2678–6 (pbk.)
1. Ireland—History—Famine, 1845–1852. 2. Famine—Ireland—Mullingar Region—History—19th century. 3. Mullingar Region (Ireland)—History.
I. Title. II. Series.
DA950.7.012 1999
941.5081—dc21

99–29357
CIP

Typeset in 10 pt on 12 pt Bembo by
Carrigboy Typesetting Services, County Cork
Printed by ColourBooks Ltd, Dublin

Contents

Acknowledgements

I would like to acknowledge the support, advice and encouragement given to me by many people during the course of my research on the Famine in the midlands. Dr. Dympna Mc Loughlin, my thesis supervisor, was always most encouraging and her advice was invaluable. Dr. Raymond Gillespie, Course Director, and Dr. Mary Ann Lyons, Acting Course Director, were both inspirational and extremely helpful. The friendship and co-operation of my fellow students in the Maynooth MA class of 1996–98 were deeply appreciated. Thanks are also due to the many libraries and archives for their help in facilitating my research; The National Archives; The National Library of Ireland; Westmeath County Library; The Royal Irish Academy; and The Library of N.U.I. Maynooth. My friends and colleagues on the Staff of Colaiste Mhuire, Mullingar, were always both interested in and supportive of my work on this project. Finally, in acknowledgement and deep appreciation of their unstinting support this book is dedicated to Marie, Aidan and Eimear.

Introduction

The sesquicentennial commemoration of the Great Irish Famine has led to a re-examination of the regional impact of what was arguably the most important watershed in modern Irish history.[1] The scale of the devastation in the south and west of Ireland has meant that its effects and consequences in the midlands and east of the country have been ignored or superficially dealt with.[2] Westmeath's location in the 'navel' of Ireland reflects the transitional territorial 'personality' implicit in its toponym.[3] The fertility of its soils and the prosperity of its agriculture can be related to its location on the rich clay plains of north Leinster. This prosperity is not evenly distributed, and it fades as the gateway to the west through the Shannon bridgehead at Athlone is approached. Thus, the compact territorial template described by Mullingar poor law union encompassed the varying economic circumstances of communities in both the east and west of Ireland.

The trilogy of people, place and time form the essential reference points for any local study.[4] People are the most important part of this triangle and as such they can only be understood in the context of the 'communities of interest' they lived, worked and died in during the Famine. As these social groupings ranged from 'peer to peasant' it would be impossible to describe the communal impact of the Famine without analysing the consequent effects on its component parts. Between the social extremes of labourer and landlord were the cottiers, small farmers and the grazier tenant farmers. Religion, politics and economic self-interest further complicated the reactions of these disparate social groups to the harvest failures and the government's relief measures. This study is a micro-regional analysis of the social and spatial effects of four consecutive harvest failures of varying intensity, of the staple food of almost 40 per cent of this union's population.

Mullingar poor law union is an ideal unit for a local study. Its compact morphology, its focus on the county town which contained the union workhouse, and its delimitation within the county boundaries reflected the poor law administrators tacit recognition of a 'community of interest' that would support its poor through local taxation (fig. 1). The unions twenty-six district electoral divisions were formed from an amalgam of townlands and as such sprang from the core communal units of mid nineteenth-century Ireland.[5] This study contextualises the Famine experiences of these micro communities within both a union and a national setting. The narrow time scale chosen facilitates the detailed analysis of the effects of the Famine in this area. However an exclusive focus on the Famine years would make such an analysis shallow and non-contextual. To provide context study examines Mullingar before, during and after the Famine.

The point of reference for the three central sections of this study is the fate of each of the Famine harvests. The crisis that followed each deficient harvest was in the first instance a traumatic experience for those most dependent on the potato. It also revealed the workings of the larger community through the fissures thus revealed. It is through these fissures that the impact of the Famine on all the 'communities of interest' is analysed.

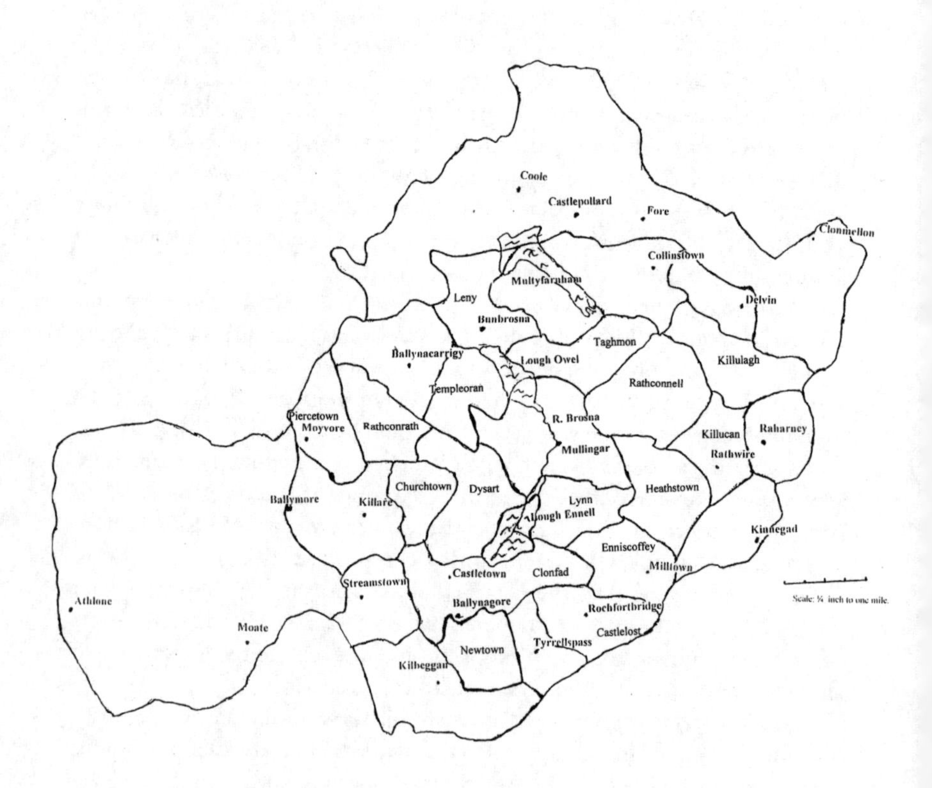

1 Mullingar poor law union, Co. Westmeath 1838–51

Mullingar poor law union before the Famine

'After breakfasting in Kinnegad we came into the great road between Dublin and Ballinasloe . . . there was little apparent improvement in the condition of the poor. The women and children were generally ill clothed the men looked worn and thin. Everywhere we saw the great coat, the long spade, the outside car, the dray, the light horse, oats, potatoes and bog.'[1]

FORMATION OF THE UNION

The site of the Mullingar union workhouse was on the northern exit from the town, along which were to be found 'many of the cabins and abodes of poverty'.[2] Being on the northern periphery of the town it was part of the newly emerging Catholic institutional quarter which evolved here following the building of the Cathedral on 'Back of the Town' street seven years after the granting of Catholic emancipation. As such, it was as far away as possible from the old establishment core of Mullingar, which evolved around the original Norman castle in Gaol Street.[3] It was also suitably distant from the picturesque demesnes, which dotted the shores of Lough Ennel to the south of the town. More significantly perhaps, it also had the advantage of a 'good quarry'; a not unimportant consideration, as the poor law required the paupers to break stones in return for food and shelter.[4]

Mullingar poor law union was one of the 130 unions into which Ireland was divided following the passing of the 1838 Poor Law Act.[5] Even though it was the tenth largest poor law division in the country in area, its population of 73,272[6] made it only the forty-second most populous. It thus reflected its geographical location between east and west, being far less impoverished than the western unions yet not quite as prosperous as the unions of the north east or the east.[7] The union described a radius of twelve miles around the central focus of the county town of Mullingar. This was the distance that a labourer and his family were expected to walk in a day to the workhouse. The board of guardians administering this midland union was evenly balanced between what the local ascendancy paper called 'the radicals'; the *ancien regime* comprising the remnants of the old Norman families like the Tuites of Sonna and the Nugents of Delvin, who had retained their estates by changing their religion, and the newer English settlers like the Smyths and the Levinges, who had benefited from the Cromwellian confiscations of the seventeenth century. The oldest Norman family in Westmeath – the Nugents of Castletowndelvin – provided the chief civil officer of the county and the union.[8] The marquis of Westmeath, George Nugent, who resided in Clonyn castle, Delvin, was the lieutenant and the custos rotulorum of the county. As such he was the most important medium of communication between the local gentry and the government representatives in Dublin castle;[9] he delegated this task to his vice-lieutenant, Sir Richard Levinge, during this crisis (fig. 2).

The post Napoleonic war slump in agricultural prices, and the deindustrialisation which followed the setting up of the factory system in England impacted most severely on the cottier and labourer class in Ireland.[10] In Mullingar union the post 1815 period saw a decline in tillage and a significant increase in pastoral farming.[11] The size of farms increased as the graziers cleared their estates of surplus tenantry to make way for the new farm enterprises.[12] Lying on the rich clay plains of north Leinster, the union was ideally situated to

2. Sir Richard Levinge

benefit from the change to pastoralism which was taking place before the Famine. The graziers farmed the best land. This group comprised landlords and the more substantial tenants whose holdings exceeded thirty acres. As these tenants held leases, they were in a position to improve their holdings and to benefit from the new agricultural methods being promoted by the Westmeath Agricultural Society. They represented the emergent Catholic middle class and were the dominant group elected to the board of guardians. However, landlords were the wealthiest farmers in this class. Richard Reynell was one of the most extensive farmers in Westmeath. By 1845, just 4.8 per cent of his 3,500-acre estate was devoted to tillage.[13] This meant that there was much less employment for labourers on estates such as Reynell's as he gave employment to just one labourer for every one hundred acres of his property.

The comparative prosperity of the union was confined to the graziers as the small farmers still relied on tillage.[14] The economic condition of the labourers and the small farmers was deteriorating before the Famine.[15] This decline was compounded by the poor harvests of 1839–41, which bankrupted many small grain producers and the labourers dependant on them for work. This minor subsistence crisis initiated a stream of emigration to New York and Buenos Aires, which was to become a torrent during the Famine and post Famine periods.[16] Despite the prominence given to large farmers at the Devon Commission which met in Mullingar in 1844, when all but one witness, David Harton, the union valuator, were graziers, the vast majority of the farmers in the union were small holders.[17] 37 per cent had between two and twenty acres while a further 41 per cent had less than one statute acre. The latter, and the landless labourers, who depended on conacre to grow their staple foods of potatoes and oats, suffered most during the Famine. The miserable cabins in which the poor resided struck even the most favourable commentators on the prosperity of this region. When the travel writer Wriothesley Noel passed through the southern part of the union along the Kinnegad–Tyrrellspass road just before the Famine, he described the living conditions of the poorest labourers and cottiers.[18] Here the mud cabins 'were in a bad condition, the windows were small holes without glass, some were without chimneys'. Inside these cabins 'an iron pot, two or three stools of the rudest workmanship, a bad deal table, a dresser with a few plates or dairy vessels were all the furniture the cottiers had. Their stock of provisions consisted of a sack of meal which was placed in a corner'.[19] 38 per cent of all houses fell into this fourth class category as they were described in the 1841 census.[20] These one roomed mud and stone cabins were the abodes of the poorest labourers and cottiers. They paid the rent of the cabin and the potato garden by working for the landlords and the tenant farmers.[21] Their wages varied from 10*d*. per day without rations in summer to 8*d*. in winter which amounted to about £10 per annum;[22] 75 per cent of these earnings were used to purchase food and the remainder barely sufficed to pay the rent.[23] The major problem facing the labourers was the lack of employment, as just 37 per cent of them had constant work; this was due to a simultaneous increase in their numbers and a decrease in the demand for their labour.[24] The majority were idle during 'the dead season' of winter and early spring,[25] as there was very little work available between 'rearing the turf' in May and the harvest in mid July. These latter 'starving summers' or 'meal months' were particularly distressful for the labourers and their families because they had to pay usurious prices for oaten meal as they awaited the coming potato crop.[26] Their food consisted of a monotonous diet of potatoes and some oatmeal, which was supplemented with skimmed milk or 'buttermilk' during the summer.[27] This dependence on potatoes rendered them vulnerable to intermittent crop failures. Similar minor subsistence crises occurred each decade from 1821 until the major crisis of 1845.[28] The fact that oatmeal formed part of the diet of the better off labourers and cottiers, as well as providing valuable income for the tenant farmers, meant that this union differed from those of the west and south west where potato monoculture was almost universal.[29] The landless labourers were dependent on the conacre system to provide their staple food.[30] The farmers let this land for a year, fully manured and ready to receive a crop of potatoes or oats. Rents at £8 per acre were extremely high yet this land was eagerly sought after.[31] In 1845, 25 per cent of all potato land in the union was held under the conacre system compared to 14 per cent nationally.[32] The poorest labourers often received conacre in lieu of wages,[33] and they used the crop from this land to feed their families and perhaps a pig, the sale of which paid the rent of their cabin.[34] They lived on the produce of the conacre when they were unemployed, which for the majority of labourers in this union was for over half the year.[35] The extent of the system in this union thus rendered its participants extremely vulnerable to the looming crisis.

However, in September 1845 such a crisis seemed remote. The workhouse had just over a third of its accommodation utilised.[36] Commercial farm enterprises had taken root in the union. It was open to innovations from Dublin with which it would soon be connected by rail.[37] The grazier and middle class farmers were prospering from the changes that were slowly taking place.[38] However the heterogeneous nature of the local economy is emphasised by the existence of subsistence farm enterprises along side the above commercial economy.[39] The landless labourers and cottiers who eked out an existence from their cultivation ridges were increasingly surplus to the requirements of the new grazier class. The potato killing fungus, *Phytophthora infestans*, which struck this union in September 1845, accelerated their exit from it by either death or emigration.

The All Absorbing Question of the Potato Disease 1845–1846

'I visited several very wretched cabins and cut open the potatoes which the people were using – without exception they were diseased – they cut away the bad parts and then pounded and boiled them with water and salt. Even in this way they can scarcely be wholesome food',[1]

The harvest reports from Mullingar in September 1845 were extremely optimistic. That initial optimism turned to despair and panic when the main crop was dug in October.[2] A large proportion was found to be 'tainted' or 'diseased'.[3] Constabulary reports estimated the loss in the union at between a quarter and three eighths of the total crop.[4] Each successive report recorded greater losses as the 'distemper' spread especially after the potatoes had been pitted.[5] Both the marquis of Westmeath and Lord Castlemaine, the most important resident landlord in the western end of the county, played down the extent of the potato failure in 1845.[6] The marquis declined to call a county meeting to discuss the crisis as this would only serve to 'raise the expectations of the people and put false notions in their heads'. He thus reflected the prevailing economic orthodoxy that the poor would exploit every opportunity to subsist on the government's munificence. Both also complained that a large proportion of the potatoes were as yet 'undug' especially those planted in the conacres.[7] These small holders would neither 'dig nor allow others to dig the potatoes' declared Richard Purdue, the proprietor and editor of the *Westmeath Guardian* because they wanted to turn the 'panic to account'.[8] The apprehension and determination of the holders of conacre is intimated by the 'Rockite notices' they posted threatening 'vengeance on landholders charging more than the ground rent' which amounted to half that contracted for. The apathy of the peasantry was also apparent from the marquis's observation that they seemed inculcated 'by a superstitious feeling that as the plague has come from providence it became them to do nothing'.[9] However this 'apathy' was more apparent than real, as the marquis expressed his alarm at their use of 'threatening language' and their reported determination 'to lay hands on anything they looked like losing themselves'.[10] The marquis's fears represented the threat the potato failure posed for the landlords and the more substantial farmers in the union, as the poorer classes would now be forced to make 'inroads' on the properties of their better off neighbours.[11] However, the local MP, Hugh Morgan Tuite of Sonna House, agreed with the landlord analysis that 'the crop had not been injured to the extent supposed' and declared that it 'was now positive that the disease was not extending'(fig. 3).[12]

These conflicting reports of the extent of the loss reflected the vested interests of the various communities in the union. The landlords and the farmers would suffer a decline in rental income if the valuable conacre crop was substantially diseased. Conversely, the labourers and cottiers were unwilling and unable to pay rents for land that had as yet produced an unquantifiable crop. In an effort to break this deadlock, rents were reduced on the conacres by 25 per cent and the marquis urged landlords to buy up any 'tainted' potatoes in 'order to put a value on them'.[13] He also wanted the workhouse guardians to install machinery to extract starch from the diseased tubers despite the fact that it was then accepted that this substance did 'not support the human frame'.[14] This confusion is not surprising as the three scientists appointed by the prime minister, Sir Robert Peel, to investigate the failure made similar suggestions.[15] When 'the indefatigable trio of potato Commissioners', as the London *Times* called them, visited Sir Richard Levinge at Knockdrin, to inquire about the extent of the loss in Westmeath, he chided them for their long and unintelligible reports, and advised them to issue simple summaries to be distributed by the constabulary, where 'there were no resident gentlemen'.[16] The scientists accepted this suggestion but their prescriptive measures failed to either cure or stop the progress of the disease.[17] However, they made a contribution to the welfare of the poor by their accurate assessment of the extent of the loss in the union.[18] Their conclusion that half the potato crop had been lost in the relatively fertile midlands was accurate but they underestimated the higher productivity of the 1845 crop.[19] Potato acreage had increased by 6 per cent in 1845 and the area planted – 12,864 acres – was never equalled before or since.[20] This increase in acreage, while ameliorating somewhat the effects of the loss, was offset by the fact that 25 per

3. Hugh Morgan Tuite

cent of the total crop was under the conacre system. It was on the tenants of these cultivation ridges that the loss fell most severely.[21]

The report alarmed the government and Peel immediately decided on a course of action that went a long way towards reducing the distress which faced the third of the population that depended almost exclusively on potatoes for their subsistence. He secretly purchased £100,000 worth of Indian corn in North America; he also set up as a new system of public works to provide employment for the thousands of labourers who would be without food or the means to procure it in 1846.[22] A relief commission was established in Dublin to organise the distribution of the Indian corn meal from the depots and to co-ordinate the activities of local relief committees.[23] The decision to establish the depot for the midlands in Longford indicated the commissioner's perception of where the greatest distress was likely to occur.[24] However this decision caused much resentment in Westmeath, as the 'lumber boats' transporting the meal to Longford passed through Mullingar. Collecting it in Longford entailed an over night stay in that town for the 'car men' from Mullingar, thus adding to the cost of the meal when it was sold to the poor.[25]

Two months after the partial failure, the panic which seized the peasantry was replaced by complacency as they realised that some form of relief would be extended to them in 1846. Sir Francis Hopkins of Rochfort, who was chairman of the Westmeath Farming Society, informed the lord lieutenant that not withstanding the 'alarming prevalence of disease'in the potatoes, the labouring population would not need help until the 'ensuing summer'.[26] Just three weeks after writing this memorial to Lord Heytesbury an attempt was made on his life by Bryan Seery as he returned home from a social evening with Col Cauldfield at Bloomfield House.[27] The attempted assassination of Hopkins outside his residence, shocked the ascendancy class, and revealed the deep divisions in the union community. In contrast to his previous reluctance to call a meeting to discuss the potato failure, Lord Westmeath immediately assembled his magistrates and deputy lieutenants in the courthouse to discuss the murder attempt. He added a footnote in his letter to Heytesbury, which stated that it 'was probable', that the state of the potato crop would also be discussed.[28]

Bryan Seery was a small tenant farmer on Hopkin's Rochfort estate. His fate typified the increasing pressures on small farmers as landlords consolidated their estates by creating larger farms. Hopkins justified his refusal to continue Seery's tenancy by citing his 'lack of capital' to run the larger forty acre farms. This refusal formed the motive in Hopkin's mind for Seery's attack on him. The conjunction of the murder attempt on a senior member of the local ascendancy and the potato failure alarmed the landlords, particularly as Seery had been evicted during a previous subsistence crisis in 1843.[29] Their decision to request a special commission to try Seery suggests their vulnerability in an increasingly hostile environment.[30] Seery's subsequent trials exacerbated the existing communal divisions. The first trial was abandoned when the two

Catholic jurors refused to convict Seery. Dr Cantwell protested to the lord lieutenant about the 'sectarian constitution' of the second jury, which found Seery guilty.[31] The power of 'the chapel house gentlemen', was apparent when Seery was publicly hung on Friday 13 February 1846. There was 'perfect stillness' on the streets, as they were deserted apart from the 1,000 police and military specially drafted in to keep the peace during the execution.[32] The Seery trial and execution was important because it symbolised the increasing pressures that the potato failure had placed on the small farmers. The landlords determination to make an example of Seery signified their insecurity in the face of both the harvest failure and the mounting disaffection of the small farmers, who were becoming increasingly surplus to the requirements of a more efficient pastoral economy. The variegated social and spatial impact of the potato failure exacerbated these divisions, particularly in the worse affected districts.

By April 1846, 45 per cent of the union's potato crop had been destroyed and the disease was still progressing.[33] The loss was not uniform and it reflected the 'checker board' pattern found all over the country.[34] People living beside each other were affected quite differently, one suffering slight loss the other losing everything.[35] Hilly areas of the union such as Collinstown, Taughmon and Killare suffered the greatest loss while the relatively flat areas of Mullingar, Killucan and Killulagh escaped relatively unscathed. This patchwork pattern of the disease seems to have influenced peoples decision to grow potatoes on hills again two years later, since the disease was felt to have preferred the lowlands.[36]

The Dublin Castle authorities used three criteria to evaluate the effects of the loss in Mullingar union – the proportion of the crop lost, the number of unemployed labourers in each district and the number of vacancies in Mullingar workhouse.[37] The first two criteria were closely related. In order to cope with the crisis George Nugent set up relief committees in nine Petty Session districts prior to his departure to his wife's home in England in February 1846.[38] These committees were composed of landlords, clergymen of all persuasions and the 'most intelligent cesspayers'.[39] They estimated the extent of local distress, raised subscriptions to alleviate this distress and issued work and meal tickets to those they deemed worthy of employment on the public works. Before his departure, the marquis instructed them to 'disabuse the peasantry of the monstrous notion' that they could get aid from the government if they had not dug and stored their potatoes as directed by the scientists.[40] However the peasantry's instinct proved correct as the potatoes left in the ridges were 'sounder and more kindly' than those stored in their cabins.[41]

The pattern of distress reflected the proportion of the crop lost in each district. However two other factors not associated with the failure – absenteeism and hoarding – added considerably to the privations of the poor. By December 1845 the commissioners were receiving reports of distress from those districts which had lost one half or more of the potato crop.[42] The nature of the distress was similar in the worst affected areas – Collinstown,

Taughmon, Killare, and the barony of Fartullagh. Large numbers of unemployed labourers and their families had to subsist 'altogether on diseased potatoes' and in many instances these supplies were 'already exhausted'.[43] Thus, in early 1846 these people were dependent on landlords or the charitably disposed as relief schemes did not come into operation until March.[44] Between them, Collinstown, Taughmon and Fartullagh had over 1,000 labourers unemployed in March 1845, representing 4,000 men women and children.[45] Killare, on the western extremity of the union, was the worst affected district with the greatest crop loss and the highest proportion unemployed. When an assistant poor law commissioner, John Ball, surveyed this area in March he visited some 'wretched cabins on either side of a flooded stream'.[46] The potatoes the people were forced to eat were among the 'worst he had ever seen' and he deemed them 'unfit for human use'. The barony of Fartullagh comprised large grazier farms and many 'resident gentlemen' lived there.[47] Because of the low population density of the rural areas and the constant employment available to the herds, distress was slight. Labourers congregated in the villages of Milltown, Rochfortbridge and Tyrrellspass and it was from these villages that the reports of 'extreme distress' came in January and February when the people were described as 'literally starving'.[48]

The usual starving summer had visited the wretched cabins of the poor some five months earlier than usual. However, just as the visitation had been spatially selective it also varied in its social impact. Sir Richard Levinge described the stockyards of the farmers as 'well supplied with corn much of which was as yet unthreshed'.[49] Ball observed similar differences in Killare. Here the Widow Lennon, a large farmer on the bankrupted Malone estate, told him that when the 'eatable portion' of her six-acre potato crop was exhausted by November 1845, she fed the diseased tubers to her cattle, even though they 'didn't thrive on them'.[50] The poor of this area were forced to share the same diseased diet as the animals. Evidence that the failure had also begun to destabilise the next stratum of the social structure in this area can be deduced from a memorial sent by the small farmers to the lord lieutenant.[51] Farming between one and four acres, they complained about the high cost of provisions and sought employment on the public works to enable them to purchase oatmeal. Just above the labouring class, and in many cases barely distinguishable from them, they now found themselves on the verge of sharing the poverty which was the lot of their landless neighbours.

The proportion unemployed in each district was especially significant following the failure. The variation in this proportion reflected the presence and activity of the local landlords. In the immediate aftermath of the failure, the government was determined that 'Irish property would support Irish poverty'.[52] Given that almost three-quarters of the population of the union was illiterate the people looked to the landlords and their clergy for relief and leadership.[53] Landlord response in this union ranged from pro-active interventionism, through espousal of *laissez faire* economic orthodoxy to the total indifference of the absentees. The simplistic model of cruel evicting landlords and a long suffering tenant and labouring class, for so long an accepted part of the Famine mythology and folk memory, is like all such models too simplistic. Landlords such as Hugh Morgan Tuite,[54] William Barlow Smythe,[55] Mrs. Cooper[56] and Charles Hamilton, agent for the trustees of Wilson's hospital,[57] all helped alleviate distress by providing extra employment. Tuite, as well as employing 120 workmen, was also instrumental in securing rent reductions on the conacres after the crop failure.[58] The marquis of Westmeath, as leader of the union gentry, tended to take a minimalist view of the crisis, seeming more concerned with the prospects of the poor making 'inroads on the property and possessions' of the better off than with the crisis facing a significant proportion of those under his jurisdiction. His marriage to the earl of Salisbury's daughter, and the attentions paid to his wife by the duke of Wellington, who was a member of Peel's cabinet at this time, may help explain his departure from Clonyn in February 1846.[59] However his departure provided a poor role model for the other landlords and led to delay and confusion in distributing government advice and assistance.[60] Thomas Uniake, of Lynnbury, represented the high Tory *laissez faire* economic orthodoxy.[61] He stated that the crisis was 'grossly exaggerated' and he deprecated government intervention in setting up 'the potato and fever' commissions.[62]

However, the greatest problem associated with the landlord system in this union was undoubtedly absenteeism. It was so bad in Killare that Ball could not think of any names to forward to the commissioners for a relief committee.[63] Absenteeism also added to the distress in Clonfad[64] Collinstown[65] and Taughmon.[66] Conditions were aggravated in Castletown and Dysart by proceedings taken against the 'luckless hirers of conacre'.[67] When they failed to pay their contracted rents of £9 per acre following the failure, Hercules Robinson, of Rosmead, sought new tenants; but even at the reduced terms of £6, £5 and £4 per acre, not 'one took a yard', because of what he termed 'a systematic combination which the dread of famine' was wholly insufficient to overcome.[68] When Sir John Nugent's bailiff, Bryan Kenny, took over some of these conacres he was shot as he travelled to his home in Balinea.[69] This outrage, the first since Seery's execution, reveals the inherent communal tension exposed by the potato failure. This tension generated by the crop failure reveals its stark reality here. Robinson complained of overpopulation on the conacre portion of his 240-acre estate.[70] Even though 180 of these acres were 'torn up' in conacres, Robinson admitted that they were all that stood between the hirers and starvation.[71] The halving of the area under conacre between 1845 and 1846, made this a choice between starvation, the poor house, and emigration for many labourers in this union in the aftermath of the subsistence crisis which commenced in 1845.[72]

Many estates were in financial difficulties in this union before the Famine. The Granard estate in Mullingar, as well as being headed by a minor, was in chancery. Bishop Cantwell used the example of this estate to contradict the Home Secretary, Sir James Graham's assertion that the landlords were relieving the distress.[73] The bishop maintained that during his twenty years in Mullingar he had not witnessed 'a day's labour or a shilling's charity' being extracted from the Granard estate despite drawing rents of nearly £6,000 per annum from the area. The importance of active, resident and solvent landlords is best illustrated by comparing Killare and Collinstown. Both suffered the same crop loss but Killare suffered far greater distress because of absenteeism and the high number of estates that were in financial difficulties in this area.

The charitable and representational efforts of clergymen were also significant in relieving the misery of the wretched cabin dwellers. Rev. William Eames had been rector of Clonfad, Tyrrellspass, for twenty years when the Famine started.[74] As a result of his persistent representations to both the Board of Work and the relief commissioners he secured funding for the construction of the 'Famine' road between Tyrellspass and Newell's bridge over the river Brosna which provided substantial employment in this distressed area during 1846.[75]

The political and religious divisions of the community were revealed by Bishop Cantwell's efforts on behalf of the poor of Mullingar. He had to avail of the legal skills of his friend, and 'Ireland's Liberator', Daniel O'Connell, in order to secure the funds of the Hevey trust from the clutches of the newly appointed charitable commissioners. As a result he felt confident that he would be able to feed and cloth 500 people during the coming and now certain famine which he expected to commence in April 1846.[76]

The employment provided by the public works and the distribution of cheap Indian corn meant that famine conditions were averted in this union during the summer of 1846. The commencement of work on the Midland Great Western railway in January 1846 also provided employment for the favourably positioned eastern districts of Raharney, Killucan and Kinnegad.[77] All were near the then terminus of this railway, the Hill of Down, which partly explains the absence of reported distress here in 1846. However, after public works had been wound up in July,[78] and the food depots closed in August,[79] reports of renewed distress reached the commissioners.[80] Labourers from Ballynagore sent a memorial to the lord lieutenant asking him to save them from the dreaded evil of a second visitation and imploring him to 'relieve us in our present distress'.[81] Three weeks after announcing the replacement of Sir Robert Peel by the Whig, Lord John Russell,[82] Richard Purdue informed his readers with deep regret that a second fearful visitation had befallen the potato crop.[83] Sir Richard Levinge travelled to Dublin to inform the commissioners of the crisis.[84] He informed them that he had not seen a healthy field of potatoes on the journey and that his neighbour Mr Reynella had ploughed up his potato field. In a short time he concluded, there would not be any potatoes fit even for pigs. The partial failure of 1845 soon paled into insignificance as the extent of the crisis now facing the poor of this union became apparent.

The Sad Diminution of Food: 1846–1847

'I have seen poor fellows on the public works patiently carving with a knife their cold dinner out of the heart of a raw turnip'.[1]

The editor of the *Westmeath Guardian*, Richard Purdue, tried to play down the crisis facing the poor of this union. He informed his readers that the country areas had not suffered as much as the areas around Mullingar.[2] However, by the middle of August it was realised that unlike 1845, when the loss was partial, progressive and variegated, the blight had now caused immediate destruction.[3] Constabulary reports from Ballynacarrigy stated that not a stalk had escaped and that the early crop was being dug with avidity and fed to pigs.[4] In Castletown Delvin, the labourers and cottiers pared off the diseased parts before the blight penetrated to the core.[5] Five sixths of the crop had been destroyed in Mullingar by mid August.[6] Despite the partial failure of 1845, total potato acreage declined by only 22 per cent in the union in 1846 thus indicating continued confidence in this staple food.[7] However this decline disproportionately reflected the labourers inability to procure seed which is indicated by the almost halving of the acreage planted under the conacre system in one year.[8] The oat harvest was also deficient on the previous years bumper harvest with the yield estimated to be a third less than 1845.[9] This meant that the alternative staple food would be in short supply and exorbitantly priced.

The new prime minister, Lord John Russell, was if anything more committed to the principles of *laissez faire* than his predecessor Sir Robert Peel.[10] He realised however that prompt action was required to meet the crisis. Consequently the recently closed public works were to be reopened and new relief committees established.[11] Lord Westmeath responded quickly to the government measures by calling a meeting of all the magistrates, deputy lieutenants and clergy of all denominations in the court house in Mullingar on 2 October.[12] As in 1845 he handed over responsibility for organising the relief measures to the vice-lieutenant, Sir Richard Levinge.[13] Levinge immediately set about organising relief committees throughout the union. These committees administered both the government's and local responses to the food crisis between September 1846 and March 1847.

Sir Richard Levinge's decision to increase the number of relief committees from nine to twenty-two in October 1846 reflected the extent of the crisis now facing the union.[14] The supply of food was the most important function of these new committees but they also prepared the labour lists, which were approved or otherwise by the Board of Works officers. The committees were constrained by the government's directive of 31 August 1846, which obliged them to sell the meal as near as possible to local market prices.[15] This was designed to protect local traders. However this policy failed to take cognisance of the changed situation as the people's staple food was no longer available in the market or in the fields, and the prices of the alternative oaten, wheaten and Indian meal reached famine levels.

The committees raised £3,477 in this union between November 1846 and March 1847 and the government gave a further £2,960, which represented 85 per cent of the local contributions.[16] Landlords were the largest individual donors accounting for one third of the total local contributions. These ranged from the biggest single contribution of £150 from the Chapmans of Killua castle Clonmellon to £1 donated by John Charles Lyons of Ledeston.[17] Areas with estates in chancery like Mullingar, or with large numbers of absentees like Castletown and Ballymore, had very low landlord contributions.[18] The vacuum created by the non-residence of the Granards in Mullingar tended to be filled by Bishop John Cantwell, much to the annoyance of the neighbouring gentry.[19] These tensions came to the surface when the Mullingar committee was being formed. Levinge and Cantwell, as the chief civil and ecclesiastical officials in the union, clashed over the composition of the relief committee after the vice-lieutenant refused entry to the bishop's nominees.[20] The regulations stated chief officiating clergymen could serve and Levinge maintained that Cantwell, being in his words rector of Mullingar, was the only one entitled to sit on the committee. Cantwell went immediately to Dublin to protest at the exclusion of his three curates. He claimed that Levinge wanted a triumph over the Catholic clergy. Routh, the chairman of the relief commission, supported Cantwell's position that his episcopal commitments were incompatible with attendance on the relief committee. The significant outcome of this power struggle between the ascendancy and the emerging Catholic leadership became apparent when Cantwell later assumed the chairmanship of the committee[21] and promised his co-operation through the services of his clergy to Lieut. Col. Archer in December 1846.[22] The alliance between the Catholic clergy and the local shopkeepers on the committee, was the embryonic manifestation of a middle class, which the Famine helped to forge. The re-run of this controversy when the new committees were being formed in April 1847 highlights the realisation by the ascendancy that the crisis represented a grave threat to their position.[23] On this occasion Cantwell castigated the 'local officials' for their 'discourtesy, indolence and bigotry' and went so far as to state that his clergy were the only 'assistance which inspired the poor with confidence'. Given the extraordinary and disinterested efforts of Protestant rectors like Eames in Clonfad, Boyd in Moyvore and Battersby in Castletown this was something of an overstatement. However being a staunch supporter of the Repeal of the Union, the bishop realised that the crisis represented an opportunity for his clergy to assume a leadership role at this critical juncture.[24] Coming so soon after the Seery trial and execution, this incident revealed yet again the inherent communal tension, which the Famine brought to the surface. The ascendancy's attempts to sideline the emergent Catholic leadership was frustrated by Cantwell's prompt action in alerting the relief commission of Levinge's attempt to exclude the Catholic curates.

Constrained as they were by the dictates of political economy, it is necessary to analyse the functioning of the relief committees following the total failure of 1846. When the meal dealers in Ballynacarrigy banded together to fix prices, the formation of a relief committee effectively broke their monopoly.[25] The committee also distributed food to the infirm and widows when the workhouse was full between mid December 1846 and April 1847 when the soup kitchens opened.[26] The Kilbeggan committee eventually succeeded in establishing a soup kitchen despite the determined efforts of the local traders who feared that it would adversely affect their business.[27] The Drumcree and Kinnegad committees set up soup kitchens long before the government scheme was established.[28] A good example of what could be achieved with judicious management can be seen in Cloghan, which was established as a subcommittee of the Knockdrin district[29] in order to bring the food nearer to the homes of the poor.[30] From an initial sum of £44, they raised sufficient funds to purchase £316 3*s*. 4*d*. worth of meal and sold it for £304 10*s*. 6*d*. with 'several gentlemen' engaged in its distribution from 8 a.m. to late in the afternoon. The united communal response to the food shortage here was further evidenced by the decision of the committee members to make their own horses and carts available to distribute the meal; the administration costs in Cloghan were consequently a mere 2.5 per cent of the total fund. The difficulties encountered by the relief committees in Ballymore and Castletown were due in part to the prevalence of absenteeism in both areas and this undoubtedly augmented the existing high levels of distress here.[31] The parish priest of Ballymore, Fr William O'Brien, had almost single-handedly organise a relief fund to help feed the almost 3,000 people who were described as being in awful distress. The sum collected included £7 5*s*. 0*d*. collected in copper at the chapel over five weeks. Even the least well off had to part with their pennies to help feed the famishing creatures that were everywhere to be seen in this area.[32] The Protestant rector of Castletown, Rev. Battersby, had to rely on a donation of £100 from his cousin in London to enable him to set up a relief fund. The village's main estate was in chancery, and the local landlord, George Augustus Boyd Rochfort, had departed to his sea-side residence in Balbriggan, shortly after the failure.[33] As a result a most trying responsibility was thrown on himself and the Catholic parish priest, Fr Byrne, which was not alleviated by the local farmers contribution of a mere £1 for every £100 rent collected. This was only enough to provide one meal per day for the 180 families without food or work in the area.

The committees fulfilled an important function by reporting local distress to the relief commissioners in Dublin. As in 1845 the impact of the failure varied socially and spatially, but unlike 1845 the total failure of 1846 had more widespread social consequences and exposed new pockets of distress especially on the periphery of the union. The immediacy of the food crisis facing the union became apparent as early as October when carts transporting meal from the Quaker milling zone along the Brosna – the Perrys in Ballynagore, the Lockes in Kilbeggan and the Goodbodys in Clara – were attacked near Dysart.[34] Animal and crop theft increased dramatically,[35] and the authorities responded by imposing severe penalties on those who were found guilty of what were essentially survival crimes.[36] Sheep stealing was an almost nightly occurrence[37] which the imposition of a dreaded seven year transportation sentence failed to stop.

Consequently the large numbers transported in 1847 reflected the intensity of the distress experienced in this union as the people desperately struggled for survival.[38] All the females transported committed survival type crime and 65 per cent of the men were found guilty of animal theft.[39] The dramatic increase in the number of prisoners in Mullingar gaol similarly reflected the mounting crisis outside.[40] The number of prisoners increased from 75 in May 1846 to 270 in June 1847 and this figure included twenty-five children who were obliged to accompany their parents into the prison. Amongst those incarcerated were a husband and wife who were sentenced to three weeks hard labour each for 'rooting potatoes'.[41] Overcrowding in the prison was caused by the number of convicts being held there in 1847 as they awaited transportation. The governor, James Tyrrell, wanted them transferred immediately to Dublin as owing to the crowded state of the prison he could not answer for their health. These measures did not stop the rising crime levels, which were directly linked to the subsistence crisis. To protect themselves and their property the farmers in Castlepollard and Mullingar purchased an immense number of guns, pistols and bayonets from a travelling vendor.[42] Such was the extent of sheep stealing in the union, that farmers frequently fired a shot or two out of their bedroom windows before they went to bed to frighten off would be thieves.[43] Some even reported robberies which hadn't occurred in order to deflect attention from their properties.[44] Others employed workmen to mind their turnips.[45]

The perpetrators of these crimes were those who had been pauperised by the loss of the potato.[46] One of the worst affected areas was Moyvore which was located on the north-western periphery of the union near the Longford border. Eleven Famine related deaths occurred here in the first three weeks of February 1847.[47] Conditions were so bad in this lawless sheep stealing area that no respectable females could be found to operate a soup kitchen.[48] The fact that there were 1,000 half acre plots in this area indicates the extent of the loss for the poorer class as well as the prevalence of subdivision and absenteeism. The local rector, Rev. Boyd of Ballinacurra house, estimated that one third of the lower class would be gone by summer.[49] Conditions were little better in nearby Rathconrath, where despite the employment of 1,250 people on the public works[50] there were 2,000 starving poor.[51] They were

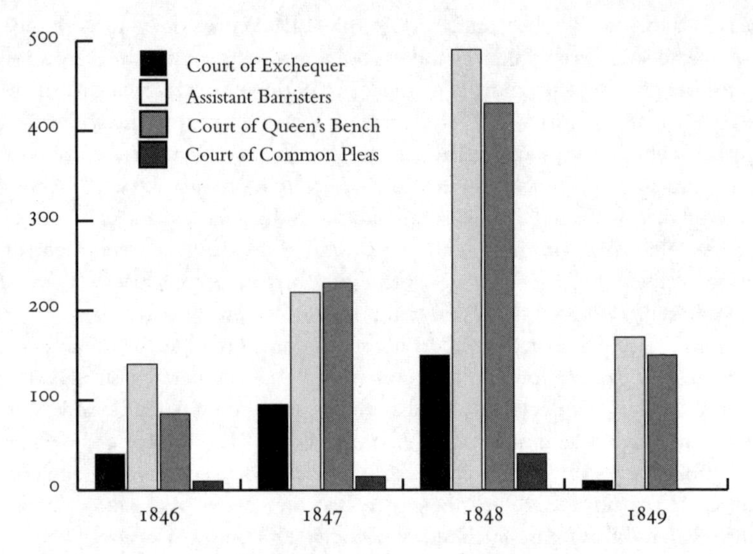

4. Evictions in Westmeath 1846–9

suffering from the effects of the starvation of the previous season and many were forced to subsist on pollard and bran, a food previously given to pigs.[52] Throughout the union generally the appearance of the population was wretched. Their clothing was in rags and fuel in many areas was not to be had because of the numbers employed on the public works the previous summer, which was the usual turf cutting season.[53] The social impact of the total failure of 1846 was much more extensive than the partial failure of 1845. In the Killare area Fr O'Brien estimated that the consecutive and cumulative losses had created 1,600 beggars there which included people who farmed up to ten acres.[54] The pauperisation of these small farmers is indicated by the fact that despite self starvation in December and January they were now forced to eat the small stocks of seed oats they were husbanding for the spring sowing.[55] This self starvation indicates their desperate attempt to prevent their descent into the poverty and destitution of the labouring class. Their pigs and poultry were gone[56] and the odd starving cow was all that stood between them and starvation.[57] This group was in a position to withstand the partial failure of 1845 by getting meal on credit during the summer of 1845.[58] The second failure effectively pauperised them as they rapidly used up their remaining resources during the autumn and winter. Those holding more than three acres had survived the partial failure of 1845. The total failure of 1846 had made those holding seven to ten acres beggars and they now craved to be on the public works as these were the only buffer between them and the ignominy of seeking admission to the workhouse like the landless labourers of their neighbourhoods.[59] The effect of the failure was also age selective and was most severely felt by the old and infirm as well as by the very young.[60] The

Ballynacarrigy relief committee supported over 100 destitute widows and orphans; old people frequently fainted in the committee rooms for want of nourishment and absolute starvation.[61]

Destitution was far from universal in this union however. The large farmers' haggards were full throughout the winter months of 1846–7.[62] Landlords realised this and felt justified in not giving those with over thirty acres rent abatements.[63] The higher prices obtained for all agricultural products at this time meant that the loss of the potato crop did not impinge significantly on this class.[64] They could feed their families from their oat crop[65] and many were members of relief committees to whom they sold large quantities of oaten and wheaten meal.[66] They thus had a vested interest in ensuring that the government directives on market prices were adhered to. Landlords suffered a decline in rental income following the failure.[67] They also suffered from the loss of the potato crop which they traditionally used to feed and part pay their workmen.[68] As a result a number resorted to clearing their estates of surplus tenantry.[69] The cumulative effects of the crop losses of 1845–6 manifested themselves in 1848 as the number of evictions peaked (fig. 4).[70]

These were particularly severe in the Kilpatrick area of Mullingar where twenty-seven families were evicted from lands belonging to the Erasmus Smith school in Oldcastle, County Meath.[71] The fact that Sir Richard Nagle's agent was a prominent local Catholic, did not protect his tenants on Carn hill and Garthy as twenty-four families were evicted in 1847.[72] Outrages which followed these evictions, were often directed against the new tenants rather than against the landlords or their agents.[73] The tenants about to be evicted did not accept their fate passively as is evidenced by a violent attack on a process server in Fartullagh.[74] The scale of the renewed strains which the failure placed on landlord tenant relations can be inferred from the fact that this official had no less than forty-nine processes in his possession when he was attacked near Tyrrellspass.

Some landlords in the union took their responsibilities as leaders of their respective communities of labourers and cottiers seriously. Hugh Morgan Tuite gave over £1,000 worth of assistance to the poor on his Sonna estate in the form of meat, clothing, money and food.[75] Mrs Cooper purchased thirteen tons of rice and Indian corn and twenty tons of breadstuffs to sell at cost price to the labourers attached to her Dunboden estate.[76] The Smyths of Gaybrook and Collinstown gave money to the poor and small farmers to help them emigrate.[77] As prices rose in January and February 1847 some landlords opened soup kitchens on their estates.[78] Absenteeism, as in 1845, augmented the existing distress in Ballymore, Moyvore, Castletown and Streamstown.[79] The situation was so bad in Castletown that 500 people had to survive on one meal a day, which consisted of turnips and pigmeal and for which they were obliged to travel several miles to Perry's mills in Ballynagore.[80] The lord chancellor's refusal of assistance from the funds of the Granard estate in Mullingar augmented the dreadful distress in the town which was due in part to the excessive amount of paupers continually flowing into it from the distressed rural districts of the union.[81] Moneys from the Hevey trust, which had helped feed and educate 500 people during the previous season were now diminished because the fund depended on rental income which had declined due to the failure.[82] The suddenness and totality of the failure meant that the most vulnerable, weakened already by the failure of 1845, suffered the consequences of this subsistence crisis.[83] The next layer of the social stratum began to experience the distress which the labourers habitually suffered each summer. Farming up to ten acres, the experience of sudden impoverishment must have been traumatic as the members of this class saw themselves as farmers and as such was quite separate from the labourers in the social hierarchy of pre-Famine Ireland.[84] The peasantry was replaced by the small shopkeepers and small farmers in the pawnbrokers shop in Mullingar as the social structures adjusted to the crisis. However a new distinction between them and the better class of farmer was created by the potato failures. The Board of Works inspector in the union noted that the bigger farmers were tilling their land in January 1847, while the holdings of the small farmers were utterly neglected.[85] Their position was precarious prior to the failures and it was now untenable as they were forced to join their landless neighbours on the public works. One effect of the blight was to redefine the term 'farmer' as it became typically associated with the larger tenants and graziers to the exclusion of those under ten acres. Immediately after blight struck the union Hugh Morgan Tuite recognised the magnitude of the crisis and, significantly, the threat posed to the propertied class by the loss of the potato crop. He informed the relief commissioners in early September that the harvest work was completed and that in order to prevent tumultuous meetings and starvation the recently closed public works should be immediately re-opened.[86] The new Labour Rate Act[87] was the Whig administration's chief response to the crisis. An indication of the magnitude of the crisis now facing this and other unions is inferred from the fact that whereas the previous Tory administration could defer the public works until March 1846, they now had to be commenced in September.[88] The labourers and cottiers immediately realised that their only means of surviving the winter months without their traditional subsistence crop was to find employment on the works. Far from accepting their fate passively, they gathered around the presentment sessions where the ratepayers decided on the extent of the proposed works. The presence of 1,500 labourers outside a presentment session in Castlepollard no doubt helped Gerald Dease announce to the cheering workers that the meeting had approved works totalling over £2,000.[89] The numbers employed on the works increased dramatically from 672 in mid October to over 4,755 by mid December,[90] which was similar to other Leinster counties but just over half the numbers on the works in neighbouring Longford thus indicating the substantial local variations in distress.[91] Within the union there were also significant spatial variations in the numbers availing of this relief. The high dependency on the works in Ballynacarrigy, Moyvore, Rathconrath and Killare is indicative of the higher relative levels of distress in these western districts of the union.[92] These figures do not fully reflect the intensity of distress however as there were more applicants than places on the works.[93]

The destitution and low levels of skill of the workers were indicated in Mullingar when the county surveyor complained that the workers were unable to pave sewers or lay 'curb stones'. The only way he could envisage spending the £200 he had in hands was to 'roll the stuff back on the hills' the workers had just excavated.[94] The most sympathetic and in many ways the most perceptive view of the plight of the workers came from a native of the union. John Keegan was an engineer with the Board of Works and he supervised the works in the western part of the union where he was born. He described the cutting down of Streamstown hill by the half starved men:[95]

> the men are put in gangs to excavate the hills and remove earth to the hollows – six to eight loosening it with picks and crowbars, four filling the barrows and four wheeling on a double run of thirty yards to the hollow.

He lamented the bad effects that the relief works and the doling out of the 'wretched Indian meal' had on the morale and feelings of the labourers.[96] The pride which in former years had made them conceal their wants, had now given way to 'a shameless clamour for relief and yellow meale'. The relief works were not enough for many old men in the area. When Keegan visited this part of the union a week later, he was told that they 'were at the point of death or perhaps in their graves'. He was astounded at the change which the potato failure had brought to the area. When he visited some years previously the people played hurling and football, or danced to the music of the blind piper of Ballinderry, John Daly, and not one of them had heard of Indian meal. Now the people seemed to have forgotten such amusements ever existed and the jollity was replaced by the 'present death like stillness and apathy'.

What was the reaction of the other communities of interest in the union to the potato failure and the relief works? When the government inspector Lieut. Col. Archer visited the union in December 1846 he was astounded at the complete cessation of all farm activities.[97] The farmers had pushed all the labourers off the farms and onto the public works. In Collinstown farmers' sons and servants sought and got work on the relief schemes.[98] This was related to their influence on the relief committees but it may also indicate genuine distress among the small farming class. Even though Archer castigated the farmers for their 'grinding grudgery' and 'exorbitant exactions' of conacre rents, the destruction of the potato crop meant that they had lost this income as well as the potato which they habitually used to feed their workers.[99] Further, the labourers' now needed monetary compensation in order to procure the increasingly expensive food supplies, and this was only available on the public works. The landlords were opposed to the public works and called for reproductive works alone such as sub-soiling and draining their estates.[100] The chief secretary, Labouchere, in the so-called 'Labouchere letter' did allow some reproductive works alongside the public works.[101] The Smyths of Drumcree and Gaybrook as well as Bishop Cantwell, who was trustee of the Hevey lands in Bryanstown, Dysart, availed of this scheme.[102] However the number of labourers relieved by this scheme was small and the really destitute in this union did not benefit from them.[103]

Drainage works also formed part of the relief scheme. All the major rivers in the union – the Inny, Brosna, Deel and the Boyne – were 'scoured'.[104] The inadequacy of the scheme was apparent in Kinnegad where employment on the Boyne drainage scheme and the rapidly progressing railroad were inadequate because they did not give employment to the old or young people.[105] The self-interest of some landlords could also frustrate the efforts of those who were prepared to undertake drainage schemes. When Mr Tighe of South Hill, Delvin, proposed a major scheme which would give employment to 900 labourers for three months he was blocked by some of the local landlords because they feared the scheme would 'interfere with their ornamental lakes'.[106] On the other hand another local landlord, Sir John Nugent, gave employment to fifty men excavating a lake in front of Ballinlough castle.[107]

How effective were the works in relieving the distress in this union? The fact that they were carried out over the short winter days and the very harsh weather conditions which prevailed during December, January and February meant that the workers found it difficult to earn sufficient wages to purchase enough of the increasingly expensive food.[108] Even with two-thirds of some families in Rathconrath on the works they still could not earn enough to cope with the high prices.[109] The poor had to struggle to maintain their position on the works as farmers in Tyrrellspass succeeded in having their horses placed on the relief schemes at the expense of the labourers' ponies and asses.[110] These works cost 75 per cent more than if completed in the normal fashion by the grand juries.[111] The general distress of the labouring population is implicit in the county surveyor's comments that the extra cost was incurred by the 'debility' of the labourers and by the numbers he was obliged to employ. However for a significant proportion of the labouring population these 'starvation wages'[112] were the only barrier between them and certain death. This harsh reality became obvious when the government decided to abandon this relief scheme in February 1847.[113] The period between the closure of the public works and the opening of the soup kitchens were the months of highest mortality in Mullingar union during 1847.[114] It was also a period of social instability as 'respectable farmers' and the 'middle class' became alarmed at the increasing number of outrages being committed.[115] When the works provided employment in December and January the people had become quieter and the higher classes resident in this area were less apprehensive.[116] Now the farmers in Castlepollard and Tyrrellspass wanted extra troops deployed to their areas because of the dangers posed by the transition from the public works to 'that of feeding the people by rations'.[117] These fears were not unfounded as Richard Reynell from Delvin discovered when between 200 and 300 men who had been laid of the works, marched on his house and demanded work and money.[118] This show of strength by the labourers frightened Reynell so much that he threatened to fire on them. They in turn threatened to kill his sheep and actually robbed a bakery he had set up in his estate to keep down prices. This episode reveals the fears of the labourers as the works were closed. It also unmasks the conventional portrayal of the peasantry as a submissive mass at the base of the social hierarchy. The propertied classes did not have the advantage of strength in numbers or the familiarity with distress, which the labourers experienced every summer, and this crisis severely threatened their peace and security.[119] In response to this threat, they urged the government to immediately open the soup kitchens in order to avert the threat of social unrest. The need for this initiative soon became apparent in Killare and Ballynacarrigy; the 'famishing creatures' who had been dismissed from the public works now faced utter destitution because the soup kitchens were not yet established.[120] It was in this disorganised and precipitous fashion that the government's main response to the failure ended. They now abandoned the policy of providing relief through employment on public works. They also divested themselves of an essential part of their economic orthodoxy by deciding to provide outdoor relief to the thousands now being laid off the works in this and other unions.

The abandonment of the public works and their replacement with soup kitchens, which would supply cooked food, mostly free, marked a significant change in government policy.[121] Even though it is generally agreed that this policy was successful, the hiatus between the closure of the works and the opening of the soup kitchens was characterised by increased distress, mortality and social upheaval.[122] The escalation in food prices meant that the labourers on the public works could not earn enough to feed their families. Bishop Cantwell responded to this crisis by abolishing the traditional Lenten restrictions on the eating of meat and eggs and he also allowed the labourers to work on holy days to enable them to earn more on the public works.[123] The government inspector, Lieut. Col. Archer, was also alert to the potential food crisis facing the union when he informed the chairman of the Relief Commission, Sir Randolph Routh, that the area's food supply would be gone by the end of spring.[124] The change in direction in the government's policy was obvious in Routh's reply. He advised Archer to call a meeting of the proprietors of the union so that they could establish food kitchens to distribute 'a cheaper kind of food'. This transfer of responsibility for relief onto the union's proprietors was also indicative of the change in relief policy. The

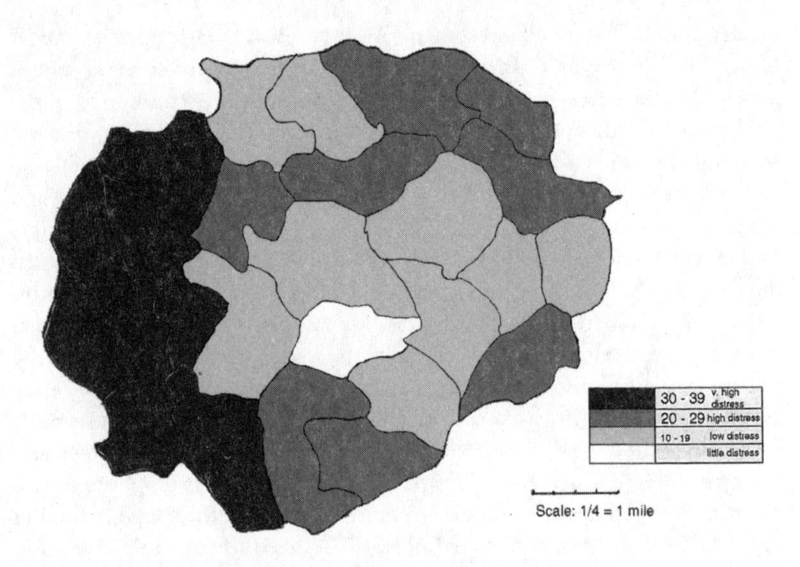

5. Variations in distress as measured by soup rations issued

government was influenced by the success of charitable organisations like the Irish Relief Association and the Society of Friends, both of which had helped set up soup kitchens in this union during the winter of 1846.[125] The Quakers established the first and prototype soup kitchen for this area in their 'little Pennsylvania'[126] of Moate, in November 1846. Dr. Bewley and the parish priest, Fr Peter Murray, set up the soup kitchen committee which raised the necessary funds; they then handed over responsibility for the running of the soup kitchen to a ladies committee. Several other soup kitchens were opened throughout the union before the government scheme came into operation in May.[127] Landlords like Mrs Cooper and John Charles Lyons fed their workers in this manner in early 1847.[128] The Rev Battersby used the £100 he received from his cousin to purchase two cows and a quantity of barley meal[129] in order to set up a soup kitchen in Castletown. New committees had to be formed to organise this relief scheme which meant that it did not become operational in Mullingar union until May.[130] This hiatus between the closure of the works and the opening of the soup kitchens caused extreme distress as is indicated by the increased mortality in both Mullingar and Collinstown during March, April and May. The success of the scheme was also indicated by the rapidly declining mortality rates after May, but this may also have been be due to the lower food prices caused by cheaper imports in the early summer.[131]

Twenty-five of the twenty-six district electoral divisions in the union availed of the soup kitchen act.[132] By June 25 per cent of the union's population was in receipt of soup rations.[133] As an indicator of the geographical distribution of distress within the union during a period of extreme scarcity, the take up figures for food rations, expressed as a percentage of the population of each district electoral division, provides a valuable insight into the spatial variations in distress across the union (fig. 5). It also provides a useful index against which distress can be measured in a national context.

Of the twenty-six district electoral divisions in the union 32 per cent experienced above average distress. However, the issue of soup rations exceeded the national average in only two areas – Ballynacarrigy and Rathconrath. An analysis of the spatial variations of distress in the union shows significant patterns. Clear concentrations emerge from a high to a very high level of distress in the west of the union with low levels in the east and centre. Eight districts – Ballynacarrigy, Rathconrath, Killare, Piercetown, Castletown, Newtown, Collinstown, and Streamstown experienced above average distress in the union. All these districts had above average population densities for the union. This indicates the prevalence of subletting, smallholdings and a dependence on the conacre system.[134] They also had below average literacy rates in both a union and a national context.[135] This was especially the case in Killare where distress was widespread in both 1845 and 1846. Literacy levels here were as low as 16 per cent, a full 11 per cent below the union mean. This criterion is a useful indicator of exposure to distress as these people were less well able to take advantage of new foods like Indian corn, avail of emigration or guard against diseases. Significantly, Killare also had 34 per cent of its houses in the fourth class category. These one-roomed mud walled cabins housed the poorest labourers and their prevalence here points to this districts relative poverty. These western districts were also distant from the railway works which provided well paid employment for labourers in the more favourably located eastern and central areas.

This analysis also shows that those areas which already experienced comparatively high levels of distress before the Famine were the areas most severely affected by the harvest failures of the late 1840s. This significant variation in distress in a comparatively small area of Ireland is one of the most notable aspects of the Famine experience in this region. The union also represents in microcosm the national experience with the western peripheral districts suffering the greatest distress. These areas in turn replicated the pre-Famine poverty typical of areas west of the Shannon where the rural economy was dominated by small farms, subsistence farming and high population densities.[136]

The soup kitchens closed in this union on 15 August 1847.[137] They are generally considered to have been a success[138] and the declining mortality rates in this union support these conclusions. The change of policy, which this temporary relief measure initiated, was also accompanied by a fundamental shift in the administration and financing of relief. The entire burden of famine relief was now transferred onto the poor law system.[139]

The Individualisation of Responsibility: 1848–1849

'The cholera was very bad at the time and I was afraid of it. We did not remain at the workhouse and we were afraid not to stop because we had no place to go to'.[1]

During the summer of 1847 Richard Purdue announced the reappearance of the Irishman's old favourite food.[2] The union's potato crop was described as blight free and prolific. However the extent of the crisis experienced in the union over the previous year was reflected in the 83.7 per cent decline in potato acerage compared to 1846 (fig. 6).[3] A total of just 1,610 acres was planted with potatoes in 1847 compared to 12, 864 acres in 1845.[4] The most distressed districts were most heavily dependent on potatoes. They were thus most severely affected by the failure of 1846, which was reflected in the

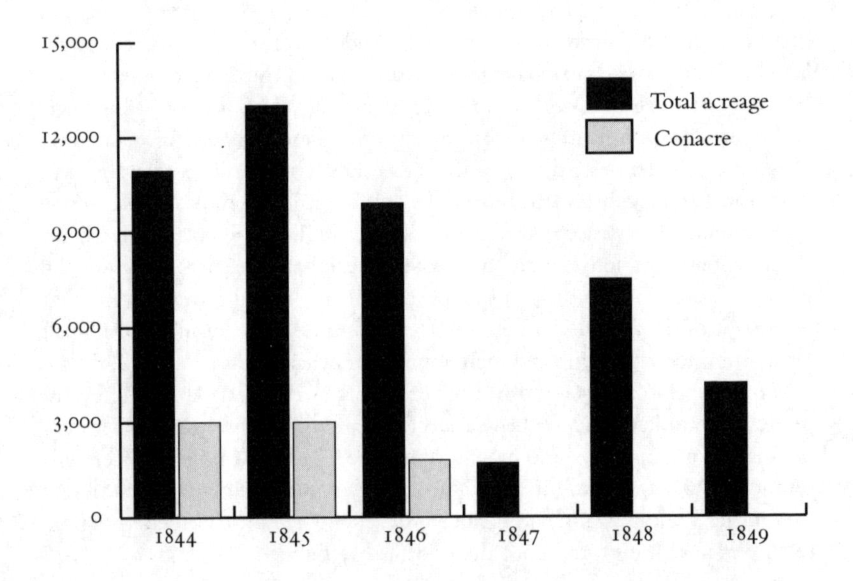

6. Potato acreage in MPLU 1845–9

comparatively lower acreages planted in these poorer districts in 1847. The decline in this union reflected the loss of confidence in the potato across the country where just 14 per cent of the 1846 acreage was planted.[5] Thus, the success of the potato harvest was mitigated by the greatly reduced acreage and the labourers, cottiers and small farmers faced yet another year of distress despite the government's declaration that the Famine was officially over.[6]

The commissioners realised that the transfer of total responsibility for the poverty of the union onto the property owners would cause problems if the rate payers had to support the 'apparent mass of destitution' which was now found everywhere in Ireland, as distinct from the utterly destitute.[7] In order to ensure that only the utterly destitute availed of workhouse relief, the commissioners advised the guardians to acquire auxiliary buildings to house the infirm and children and thus make space available in the workhouse for able bodied paupers. It was correctly concluded that this workhouse test would mean that only those suffering extreme distress would submit to it.[8] After the harvest, the numbers seeking admission to the union house soared with an average of 100 presenting themselves when the guardians met each Tuesday.[9] The extra responsibilities placed on the poor law system became apparent immediately as the guardians were forced to meet twice a week to process the applicants for admission.[10] The guardian's decisions now reflected the tensions, conflicts and accommodations between property and poverty, which the Poor Law Extension Act helped bring into sharp focus.[11] Their only acquiescence to the commissioner's request to provide additional accommodation was their decision to convert the attics of the male dormitories into sleeping quarters for 120 extra paupers.[12] Initially, the guardians contemplated doubling the capacity of the house by extending the male and female wings and building sheds for 500 children, but they deemed the cost to the ratepayers excessive.[13] Significantly they looked with renewed confidence to the next potato crop which they hoped would obviate any need for extra accommodation. Thus there was a strong connection between the success or failure of the potato harvest, the morphology of the workhouse and the level of poor rate struck in the union.

The failure of the guardians to make adequate provision for the numbers now dependent on the poor law system came to a head two days before Christmas 1847, when 1,000 paupers gathered outside the workhouse demanding immediate relief.[14] When the guardians acquiesced to their demands and allowed the relieving officers to give them provisional relief the crowd started 'cheering loudly'. Therefore, despite the cumulative effects of three consecutive years of distress the poorest people were still cognisant of the threat they posed to the propertied class. This lobbying for relief by 13 per cent of the town's population indicates a communal consciousness of their distress, as well as a degree of organisation and an awareness of their power not usually associated with the poor in Ireland. Immediately after this show of strength by the paupers, the commissioners' inspector, Mr Flanagan, authorised the provision of outdoor relief in this union. The numbers on outdoor relief rose from 4,308 in January to 8,389 in April and they reflected the level of distress here following the deficient harvest of 1847.

The heaviest reliance on this form of relief occurred in April when 11.4 per cent of the union's population relied on this form of assistance.[15] This was under half those relieved under the soup kitchen act and as such indicates the relative easing of famine conditions. Killare was again one of the worst affected districts with over 20 per cent of its population on outdoor relief. The cost had to be paid out of the poor rate, which was declining as the numbers availing of outdoor relief increased. The guardians were forced to borrow from the local National Bank and the union debt mounted from £1,000 in February to £6,000 in May. These developments alarmed the commissioners and they sent an assistant commissioner, Captain Telford, to Mullingar to investigate the affairs of the union. Telford was familiar with this midland county, as he had helped administer the Labour Rate Act here in 1846–7. From his arrival on 9 February to the dissolution of the board on 3 May he had nothing favourable to say about either the guardians or the paid officials. His main criticisms centred on the inefficiency of the rate collectors, the guardian's unwillingness or inability to enforce a test for able-bodied paupers and their failure to strike a rate, which took cognisance of the new responsibilities, which the poor law now had to carry.

The friction between the commissioners and the board, as mediated through Telford, reflected the heightened tensions between the union's various communities of interest, which became manifest as the entire responsibility for local poverty was transferred onto local property.[16] These tensions came to a head when the commissioners dissolved the board in May.[17] The increasing indebtedness of the union was one of the early symptoms of the emerging problems. The expenditure necessitated by the provision of outdoor relief as well as the inability of the small farmers in the poorer districts to pay the poor rate caused the shortfall.[18] It also reflected the government's policy of individualising responsibility. This meant that the individual property owners in the union would now have to bear all the cost of supporting the destitute in this area. This was not a significant burden during 1845 and 1846, because the public works and the soup kitchens were financed in the first instance by the government. The decision to individualise responsibility on the ratepayers caused considerable hardship, particularly in the poorer areas, where famine conditions continued, despite the government's official declaration that it was over.[19] The ratepayers, although representing the wealthier sections of the union community, were far from being a homogenous group. They ranged from the newly impoverished smallholders on the western periphery of the union who were in arrears with their rent[20] and their rates, to the large grazier proprietors around Mullingar, who paid their rates and favoured the replacement of guardians with paid officials.[21] The preference of the landed proprietors for paid officials is understandable as they were mainly ex-officio guardians and they disliked the extra responsibilities placed on the board. They may also have been influenced by the new theories which envisaged the able-bodied paupers forming a valuable pool of cheap labour which could be drawn upon at harvest time while they were supported on the rates during the winter.[22] This development threatened the livelihood of the independent labourer, but it is evidence of the increasing use of the poor law as an instrument of social and economic policy.[23] The independent proprietors also resented the liberality with which the elected guardians, who were mostly large tenant farmers, interpreted the poor law provisions.[24] Since this latter group had more contact with the distressed labourers and cottiers they were under pressure to offer them relief.[25] The landed proprietors also had to bear a larger share of the tax burden, especially in the poorer and more populous western districts, where they were liable for the rates of those whose property was under £4 valuation. The marquis of Westmeath represented the views of these proprietors and he favoured the replacement of the local guardians with paid officials whom he accurately predicted would be much stricter in their interpretation of the poor law. Implicit in this analysis is the hidden power of the labourers and cottiers who were in a position to dictate to some extent the relief policies pursued by the guardians previous to their dissolution.

The effect of the continuing distress on the small farmers was apparent in their inability to pay the poor rates or provide employment for the labourers. The labourers depended on seasonal employment and potato conacre, both of which were provided by the small tillage farmers. The concurrence of the abolition of the Corn Laws with the loss of the potato, was a double blow from which many small farmers and labourers failed to recover. The disarray of the small farming class is intimated by the union valuator's desperate efforts to rectify the many changes in occupancy, which remained undocumented in the rate books.[26] When Telford arrived he found eight pauper boys in the relieving officers room, the clerks office and the board room assisting Harton update the rate books as many small holders were either deceased or had 'quitted' the country. The large tracts of land which now remained uncultivated and untenanted was further evidence of the continuing destabilisation of this class.[27] They also lived in the highest rated districts, where absenteeism and subdivision were the norm. When Telford visited these districts in February and March 1848 he found their haggards empty and the farmers themselves were dispirited.[28] Those farming five to ten acres were placing all their hopes on the success of the coming harvest, as many of them had sold their only cow in order to purchase seed.[29] The Gregory clause destabilised them further. Whereas they could avail of relief under the Labour Rate Act and the soup kitchen act in 1846–47, the so-called Gregory clause prohibited any relief unless they surrendered their overplus to the landlord. The legal decision to allow relief to the wives and children of these small holders had the effect of breaking up their families.[30] Some small farmers in the western part of the county actually died of starvation rather than surrender their land and enter the workhouse.[31] The small farmers, whose property valuation was over the £4 valuation threshold, also found themselves in an unfavourable position in relation to the graziers under the provisions of the amended poor law. They were levied at the same rate as the graziers but this failed to take account of their higher labour costs, as the small holders were mainly tillage farmers.[32] The arrival of the steam train and the abolition of the Corn Laws further enhanced the position of the graziers. The poor law, by failing to differentiate between the two groups, accelerated the transition to pastoral husbandry in Mullingar union.[33] The small farmers had neither the capital nor the land necessary for this type of enterprise.[34] The other major cause of the union's mounting insolvency was the guardian's inability or unwillingness to insist on task work in exchange for outdoor relief. Just six out of the twenty-six districts implemented the commissioner's directive on this issue.[35] The most influential landlord in the union, H.M. Tuite, was totally against task work and he did not share the commissioner's views that the labourers abused the relief schemes.[36] He feared the consequences of large groups of labourers gathered together in quarries breaking stones where their sense of grievance could be worked on by demagogues whose 'tongues were more active than their hammers'. Tuite was an astute observer of the labouring population because of his 'personal acquaintance' of them over thirty years. When Telford continued to insist on task work an elected guardian, Thomas Glennon, warned him to 'take care travelling home'. Allied to this threat of intimidation was the guardian's refusal to increase the meal rations commensurate with the commissioners' recommendations for labourers engaged in task work.[37] Consequently the guardians were not in a position to enforce task work. The numbers in receipt of outdoor relief broadly reflected the level of distress of the poorer classes in each district.[38] The western districts were again the worse affected areas and Telford attributed this to subdivision and non-residence.[39] The beneficial effect of the employment generated by the construction of the railway between the Hill of Down and Mullingar at this time, is evidenced by the virtual non-reliance of the labouring population of these eastern districts on this form of relief. These labourers were relatively well off as meal was very cheap at this time.[40] However the unemployed labourers had to depend on the poor law. Their antipathy to indoor relief became obvious in 1848 when many of them 'indignantly' refused the workhouse test.[41] Three-quarters of those presenting themselves at the workhouse often refused to enter it hoping to get out door relief instead. The guardians' failure to enforce the workhouse test was partly due to their failure to acquire additional accommodation. It was also indicative of their fear of the reaction of the labouring population to such an unpopular policy.[42] They were also aware of the utter destitution of the poorest labourers who were now unable to cultivate their gardens, as they had no seed.[43] The Westmeath Farming Society tried to increase employment for these labourers by encouraging the farmers to revert to 'spade husbandry'. The society cancelled its traditional ploughing competition and offered instead gold medals to farmers who tilled the greatest extent of land in the traditional manner. The failure of this initiative showed the farmers unwillingness to increase their labour costs, even in these distressed times.[44] More ominously for the labourers it also indicated that they were indeed 'redundant' to the local economy. For many of them the choice now was between accepting the workhouse test, emigration or starvation.

The commissioners realised that the guardians were unwilling to face up to these realities.[45] Accordingly, after just a decade's administration by elected and appointed guardians the union was placed in the hands of two vice guardians on 5 May 1848.[46] Telford read the commissioner's letter of dissolution to the few 'astounded' guardians present that day. Most of the other guardians were either at the cattle show in Dublin, the local fair or the chairman, John Charles Lyons's horticultural show at the court house. At a subsequent protest meeting in the courthouse the loudest cheers were reserved for Tuite's claim that the real reason for their dissolution was the guardians refusal to implement the 'starvation policies' of the commissioners.[47] While there was an element of truth in this populist response, the guardians' motives were not entirely altruistic. The period between September and May, represents a transition from the caring paternalism epitomised by Tuite, to the policies about to be pursued by the vice guardians, which addressed the harsh realities of the distressed population entirely within the confines of the workhouse test.[48]

The administration of this union by the two new vice guardians, Ward and Dillon, reflected the commissioners acceptance of Telford's analysis of the problems that led to its bankruptcy; it also reflected their aloofness from all the communities of interest in the union. As a result their twelve months stewardship was characterised by policies which were at once mechanistic and ruthlessly efficient. They immediately set about rectifying the insolvency of the union by appointing new and better-paid collectors in the western districts.[49] Symbolising their determination to implement the government's new policy of making the workhouse the focus of all the relief measures, was their decision to enclose the workhouse grounds with a five-foot wall.[50] However their most significant move in this direction occurred when they hired buildings in Mullingar to house the old, the infirm and children. A disused brewery on the main street was acquired by the vice guardians five weeks after their arrival in Mullingar. Five hundred children were then transferred from the union house to the brewery, which now functioned as an auxiliary workhouse. This decision enabled them to enforce the workhouse test for able-bodied paupers. A fortnight after the opening of the brewery auxiliary, 600 able-bodied paupers were struck off outdoor relief because they refused to submit to the indoor test.[51] The decline in the numbers availing of outdoor relief partly reflected the vice guardians' determination to test destitution and to make the union house in reality a workhouse for the able-bodied paupers in this union.[52] While it had the desired effect of reducing substantially the numbers seeking relief under the poor law in this union, it increased significantly the distress of those who in the vice guardians' words 'would rather die of starvation than accept indoor relief'.[53] This choice became a reality for the poorest class in the union as the hopes vested in a successful potato crop were dashed.[54] The failure was 'quite general' across the union and Tuite estimated that the loss was as bad as 1846.[55] Westmeath was in fact one of the worst affected areas in the country, which was soon reflected in its high mortality rates.[56] Compounding the inevitable distress, which the loss of the potato entailed for the labourers and cottiers, were the poor wheat and turnip crops.[57] Both crops had been adversely affected by the extremely wet summer of 1848, as had the turf harvest.[58] Whereas the large tenant farmers were insulated somewhat from the worse effects of the previous failures by the high prices they obtained for their agricultural products, the decline in the price of cattle and sheep coupled with the poor harvest led to a sharp decline in their incomes.[59]

Despite the economic crisis now facing all sections of the union community the vice guardians pursued the policies they initiated in May. A new poor rate was struck in November to finance the increased demand for relief following the potato failure and to repay the debt incurred by the old board.[60] This was in addition to the substantial rate struck in March by the old board. Together these two rates raised £34,000 from the ratepayers. This increased taxation fell most severely on the small farmers who had 'speculated heavily' on a successful potato harvest. Their despair and disillusionment was apparent to the judges of the Westmeath Farming Society as they toured the county in the autumn of 1848.[61] Their farmsteads were 'slovenly attended' to and all the potato fields were overrun with 'rank and poisonous weeds', because the farmers had abandoned them after the failure. This despondency was also in evidence in Mullingar; when the Midland Great Western's first train arrived in the town, on 2 October 1848, it was ignored by the townspeople despite Purdue's claim that it would bring 'civilisation, trade and commerce' to the region.[62] The fact that two local landlords, G.A. Boyd Rochfort and Sir Percy Nugent MP, were directors of the company and were present on the first train, failed to excite any 'curiosity among the peasantry' and not even 'a cheer' was given to welcome the directors or the train. This lack of enthusiasm was symptomatic of the general air of depression in the town as its cabin suburbs teemed with 'squatters' who were fleeing the impoverished western districts.[63] It also probably reflected the disappointment of the unemployed labourers now that work on the railroad had ceased. The appearance of the peasantry also revealed the combined effects of four years of potato failures.[64] The deterioration in the clothing of the poor cottiers who farmed between one and five acres was particularly noticeable. The churches were 'comparatively deserted' because this class's Sunday best had been pawned.[65] The fine social distinction between the labourers and the cottiers, often symbolised by the latter's possession of a good frieze coat, was effectively eliminated by the latest harvest failure as both groups were now impoverished. The vice guardians admitted that the ending of outdoor relief contributed to the impoverishment of both groups. However any consideration of the deleterious effects of this policy were superseded by their determination to make the funds of the union defray the costs of the union. Thus the government's covert policy of using the poor law to effect social and economic change was bearing fruit as the 'redundant population' who could afford to, left the union.[66] The vice guardians' analysis of the effects of the failures on this area was accurate. The predominantly pastoral nature of the economy meant that it was not as severely affected as other areas. However the impoverishment of the small farmers meant that they could not pay their rents. This in turn meant that the means of the proprietors and occupiers in the poorer areas were 'exhausted'. Their statement that there was no opposition to the payment of rates was either deliberately mischievous or indicative of their insulation from the ratepayers.[67] The arrival of the vice guardians marked the beginning of a realisation by the landlords that the poor law extension act had in fact made them responsible for the poverty of this area. They became increasingly disaffected with, and alienated from, the government. Even though many landlords welcomed the appointment of paid guardians, they now found themselves powerless to influence the direction of poor law policy in this union and increasingly perceived themselves as the helpless victims of government 'misrule'.[68] The vice guardians were unaware of or ignored this discontent. They imposed a second rate in November, which was followed by a special levy on richer areas like Mullingar, to help poorer unions in the west of Ireland. This Rate-in-Aid caused bitter resentment especially when the Imperial exchequer was exempted. The Westmeath high sheriff, James Middleton Berry, responded to the ratepayer's anger by calling a special meeting, which took place in Mullingar courthouse at the end of January 1849.[69] The ostensible purpose of this meeting was to petition parliament to alter the poor law because the 'county had been brought to the edge of destruction by its operation'. However it expanded into a critique of the effects of the Act of Union on this region and such was the discontent of the ratepayers over the operation of the poor law that they united in condemning the government for their 'long continuous misrule' since 1800.[70] The ratepayers suppressed their religious and political differences now that they shared a common grievance. The fact that they worked together to formulate a common strategy is indicative of the combined effects of the failures, especially that of 1848, on the local economy as well as their shared dissatisfaction with the government's response to these failures.

Despite the outward show of unity, tensions surfaced between the graziers and the tillage farmers over the need to equalise taxation. The strongest criticisms were reserved for the absentee landlords, and by extension the government, for its failure to individualise responsibility on these proprietors. How important was this meeting in the courthouse? The community leaders' acknowledgement of the unique sense of unity which had been forged by opposition to the excessive poor rate only served to emphasise the heightened tensions that now existed between the ratepayers and the ever increasing community of paupers, who were now being housed in and around the town. Following so closely on their 'agitation' for rotatory parliaments the prominent part played by the gentry in formulating the petition, in co-operation with the local Catholic curate, suggests their sense of abandonment by the government. More significantly however the unity forged in the courthouse symbolised the permeating effects the repeated potato failures and the collapse in cattle and sheep prices had on the richer class in the union. The 1848 failure caused the largest single decline in landlord income in this union.[71] G.A. Boyd Rochfort's rental income declined by 61 per cent in 1849 compared to a drop of 37 per cent in 1847. When the poor rates were 'piled' on top of these misfortunes, this class and the larger tenant farmers were exposed for the first time to some of the chill winds of the Famine, which had blown through the increasingly threadbare rags of the labourer's and cottiers for the previous four years. The consequences for some of these ratepayers were obvious to the protesters in the courthouse. Many farmers were already emigrating. Some of the proprietors present would be forced to sell to English 'capitalists' at one third of what they would have got four years previously.[72] Implicit in the seeming resignation with which these changes were accepted was a realisation that these now precipitous changes were long in gestation.

Despite the vice guardians' assurances to the commissioners that there was no opposition to the payment of rates they were obviously aware of the financial constraints within which they had to operate if they were to succeed in returning the union to solvency. It is in this context that their decision to deal with all distress by means of indoor relief alone must be understood. The utterly destitute were thus caught between the government's decision to individualise responsibility and the guardians' determination to implement this policy within the constraints of the local economy. When the ratepayers gathered in the courthouse over 2,000 paupers had accepted indoor relief in the union house and its auxiliaries. A disused grain store beside the Royal Canal now housed over 100 infirm females. Infirm males were transferred to Rathconnell house, a large farmstead two miles north east of the town. Consequently the guardians were able to implement the key element of their policy of making the workhouse available to all able-bodied paupers seeking relief. Their ruthless adherence to this policy combined with their success in collecting the substantially increased poor rates enabled them to hand over a solvent union to the newly elected guardians when their term of office expired in April 1849. Their success in paying back the £9,000 loaned by the government for the soup kitchen act as well as the £6,000 debt is indicative of the relative wealth of this union. Co-existing with this wealth was a pauper population, which bore the brunt of the vice guardians' decision to discontinue outdoor relief. The pressure to return union finances to solvency took precedence over the need for a more humane response to the distress of the utterly destitute after the latest potato failure. The significantly increased mortality and the increase in famine induced diseases are the flip side of the vice guardians' successful financial management of the union affairs between May 1848 and April 1849. Their decision to hire buildings in Mullingar meant that the most destitute portion of the union population was now housed in and around the town. The workhouse inmates now comprised over one third of the town's population and as such was an important source of income for the merchants who supplied its needs.[73] However the doubling of the numbers relieved in the union house and its auxiliaries in the six months since the termination of outdoor relief in September 1848 gave credence to Sir John Nugent's observation that these were not 'ordinary times' in this union (fig. 7).[74]

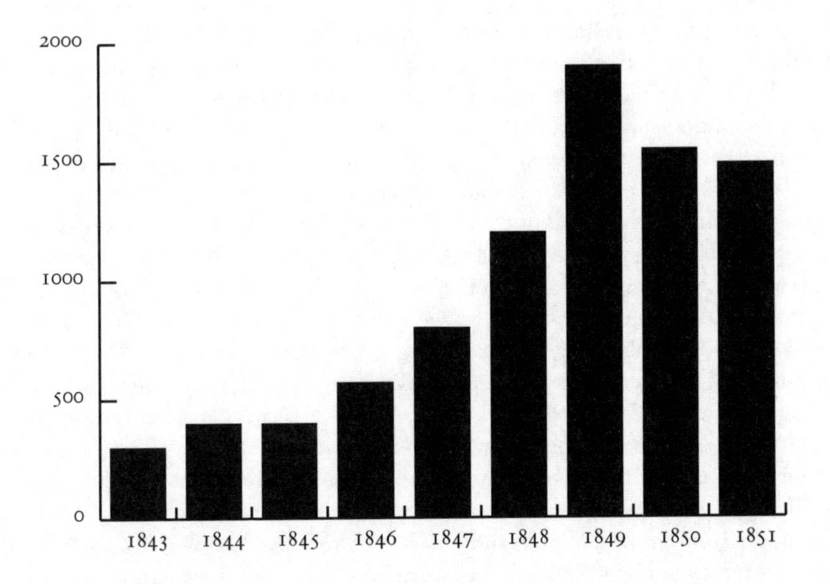

7. Number of paupers in Mullingar workhouse 1843–51

The doubling in demand for workhouse relief during 1849 indicated both the effects of the latest potato failure and the fact that this was now the only form of relief available to the distressed population. As in previous years the worst affected area was the western small farm zone which was now also the heaviest rated district in the union.[75] The poor rate of seven of these districts was over 5*s*. in the pound which placed them among the highest rated areas in the country thus giving credence to Tuite's observation that in many respects these areas were not dissimilar to large areas of the west of Ireland.[76] So many paupers were now entering the workhouse from these districts that the guardians considered hiring auxiliaries in Ballynacarrigy and Streamstown.[77] However it was deemed preferable to have the auxiliaries as near as possible to the 'parent' establishment.[78] These subsidiary workhouses were the cornerstones of the vice guardians' determined policy of offering relief only to those who submitted to the indoor test. They housed over half of those who availed of this relief between May 1848 and July 1849. These derelict commercial and industrial buildings were unsuited to the uses they were now put to. Hevey's brewery on Linen Street had fallen victim to Fr Mathew's successful temperance campaign. It had no exercise ground and its small confined yard was full of 'rusting tools' used on the roads works in 1847.[79] Nevertheless almost 1,000 juvenile paupers were packed into it by Christmas 1848.[80] Not surprisingly discipline was difficult to maintain in such overcrowded circumstances. Mr O'Driscoll, the schoolmaster in charge of the Brewery, was accused of 'attempted familiarity' and 'repeated intemperance' with one female pauper.[81] Her compelling evidence was rejected by the guardians, and Purdue's dismissal of the 'mere assertion of a pauper' as sufficient evidence, reflected the inferior status associated with these paupers, particularly the young females among them.[82]

Conditions in the Rathconnell house auxiliary were also spartan.[83] Old infirm men were transferred here in such numbers that the stables had to be used as sleeping quarters. The old men had to drink bog water because the owner, Mr Adams, would not allow them cross his land to fetch water from a spring. It was impossible to heat this old rambling farmstead with the wet turf provided by the guardians. The Dublin Bridge auxiliary had functioned as a grain store before being requisitioned by the vice guardians.[84] Between November 1848 and September 1849, when the transport entrepreneur Charles Bianconi purchased it, it was used by the guardians to house old infirm females, cholera patients and children.[85] However, the Irishtown auxiliary, which was acquired by the newly appointed guardians in June 1849, was the most overcrowded and uncomfortable of these satellite institutions.[86] The commissioner's inspector, Mr Flanagan, condemned it as quite unsuited to the use it was now put.[87] One hundred and thirty-five male and female children aged between five and ten years were housed in this byre type farmhouse. The girls were housed in the barn section which 'offered little protection' against wind or rain. The guardians protested to the commissioners that all the available houses in the town were used up. The £10 per annum rent paid to Charles Levinge for the use of this house and its proximity to the parent establishment superseded any considerations of its suitability or otherwise as an auxiliary.[88]

In many respects the county gaol in Mullingar functioned as a fifth auxiliary following the 1848 crop failure. Some poor people preferred it because of its superior food rations.[89] Built to accommodate 150 prisoners in 1828, it contained twice this number in 1849.[90] Following the failure of 1848 most of those imprisoned had committed 'petty larcenies and robberies' which were typical of the survival type crimes associated with famine conditions. Michael Kelly was jailed for robbing bread in Moate. Before dying from dysentery in the gaol he told his fellow inmates that he had frequently committed this crime.[91] Many poor people from around Mullingar were imprisoned for 'rooting' the 1849 potato crop.[92] Two wards were added to the gaol infirmary because most of the prisoners being admitted were suffering from dysentery caused by 'cold and the want of proper food'.[93] The female prisoners had to be housed in an 'ill constructed wing' of the old eighteenth-century gaol.[94] Many of those sentenced to transportation for animal theft following the 1846 failure were still in the gaol awaiting transfer to the convict depots in Dublin and Spike Island and thence to the penal colony. Ironically the opening of the Mullingar terminus of the Midland Great Western railway meant that these convicts were now being transferred to Dublin on the same trains as the graziers' cattle and sheep.[95] When used as an index of famine induced poverty, the overcrowded prison and its sickly inmates suggested to contemporaries that 1849 was the worst year of the Famine in this area.[96] The overcrowded and insanitary conditions evident in the auxiliaries were symptomatic of the extra responsibilities placed on the poor law. The fact that these conditions were endured reflects the guardians' decision to house the most vulnerable paupers in the auxiliaries. Those most likely to challenge these conditions were housed in the workhouse where the work regime could be used to enforce discipline.

However these conditions may not have shocked the paupers unduly as many had left or had been evicted from fourth class houses that were considerably worse than either the auxiliaries or the gaol. Such was the destitution of some of the poorer classes that they actively sought transportation to escape from the poverty that surrounded them here.[97] Others used the workhouse during the winter months as they awaited relatives' remittances, which would enable them to emigrate during the following spring.[98] The government scheme of assisted emigration enabled 100 female orphans from this union start a new life in Canada.[99] The carpentry shop in the workhouse provided them with specially made 'emigrant boxes' and the guardians gave them money to meet their initial expenses. The success of this policy encouraged others to enter the workhouse in the hope of benefiting from this 'El Dorado'. Some 'healthy looking females' and their children attempted to use the workhouse during the 'hungry months' of June and July while their husbands worked in England or on the recommenced railway. However exceptional these attempts at imposition may have been, they suggest that the workhouse was also used by the poor as a means of coping with temporary distress.

The vice guardians' application of the indoor test for all able-bodied paupers meant that the union house became in fact a workhouse during 1849. One of the busiest enterprises of this new work regime was the carpenter's shop, which had processed 32,911 feet of timber into 616 coffins between January and September 1849. This statistic indicates the very high mortality experienced in this union following the loss of the 1848 potato crop. It is a more accurate measure of distress than the numbers availing of workhouse relief because of many people's 'repugnance' towards this form of relief.[100] Excess mortality was higher than in 1847 and Westmeath had the second highest mortality rate of all the Leinster or Ulster counties.[101] This in turn reflected the almost total destruction of the potato crop in this county compared to the partial losses experienced in other regions. This areas high mortality in 1849 was similar to that found on the impoverished western seaboard. Apart from the cholera epidemic, which claimed eighty-three victims in the workhouse during April and May 1849, all the increased mortality was Famine related.[102] It has been estimated that between 3 and 3.9 per cent of the union's population died in 1849 as a result of the loss of the 1848 potato crop. Only four other counties in the country exceeded this excess mortality during 1849.[103] There is also evidence to suggest that reliance on the poor law to relieve distress in 1849 contributed to this higher mortality. There was one death for every thirteen

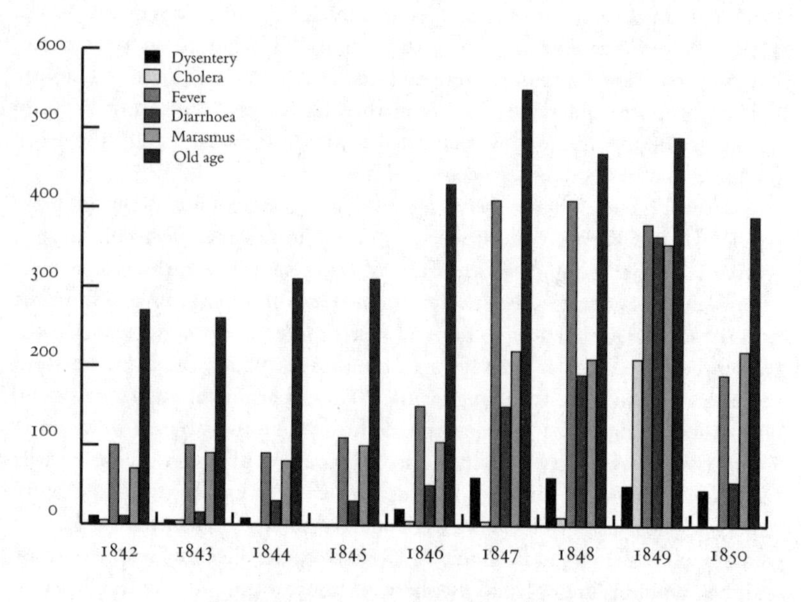

8. Major causes of death in Westmeath 1841–51

paupers in the workhouse in 1847 during the period when the soup kitchen was in operation compared to one death for every six paupers during 1849 when all distress was processed through the workhouse.[104] The contextualisation of this greatly increased mortality is best illustrated by comparing the fifty deaths which occurred in the workhouse during the twelve months preceding the end of March 1846 with the 423 deaths which occurred there in the six months following the 1848 failure.[105] Deaths directly attributable to the potato failure increased dramatically during March 1849. The age specific effects of the Famine was indicated by the very high mortality experienced by the under fourteen age group. Fifty-two per cent of all the deaths were in this age cohort and all were caused by famine related diseases like marasmus and diarrhoea. More significantly perhaps, the mortality of able-bodied paupers had increased and by March it was similar to that experienced by the old and infirm. Whereas the old and infirm suffered greatly in 1847, the able-bodied labourers were in many respects the victims of both the crop failure and the guardians' refusal to finance the cost of outdoor relief during 1849; this was reflected in the decline in deaths from old age in 1849, and an increase in deaths from diarrhoea and Marasmus, both of which were major causes of death among the labourers (fig. 8).

The able-bodied pauper's 'repugnance' towards indoor relief was evident from the fact that they were all admitted to the workhouse in 'dying state'. On St Patrick's Day, three of them were admitted in this state. One died while being carried up the stairs and the other two shortly afterwards.[106] Denis Megaley, a thirty-six year old labourer from Ballynagore, typified in many respects the distress experienced by this class in 1849.[107] He worked on the railroad and the Brosna drainage works during the early years of the Famine; both of these were at a standstill at this time. Consequently he had to seek indoor relief for his wife, his three children and himself in the union house on 26 March 1849. Because of the high mortality, which was partly caused by the outbreak of cholera in the workhouse, they discharged themselves three weeks later. Unable to find work outside the house they were forced to seek indoor relief again. However, because they sought admission before the requisite month had elapsed since they had discharged themselves, they were obliged to leave the workhouse and return to their cabin in Ballynagore despite the fact that their children were 'sick with measles'. The sick children were refused admission because their parents did not accompany them and one of them subsequently died. Three days later Denis Megaley was found dead on the side of the road near his cabin in the village. The coroner's inquest found that the cause of death was 'want of a sufficiency of food for a considerable time past'. A subsequent inquiry exonerated the workhouse authorities, the only criticism being that they should have registered the family when they stayed in the probationary ward awaiting the vice guardians' decision on their second request for relief. As well as illuminating the plight of the labourers and their families this vignette reveals the vice guardians' bureaucratic response to the considerable pressures being experienced in the house at this time as mortality and pauper numbers soared. They responded to this crisis by introducing soup and rice into the workhouse diet and acquiring a union graveyard one mile east of the house in Robinstown.[108] Mortality decreased when the food rations were improved thus indicating that the indoor test was contributing to the high death rate. The opening of the union graveyard in March indicated the severity and nature of the distress now afflicting the poorest class. Sixteen paupers were engaged full time burying the dead and one grave was left 'ready made'.[109] The low priority afforded pauper burials is suggested by the use of a boggy field, where water was found at three feet, as the union graveyard.[110] The arrival of Asiatic cholera in the town in April caused Purdue to ask 'when this pestilence hovering over our town' would vanish.[111] Though not directly caused by famine conditions, all but one of its 128 victims lived in the cabin suburbs of Cabbage Street or in the Workhouse. The one broken down pump and the general filthy state of the workhouse grounds contributed to the high mortality that accompanied the cholera epidemic which raged in the town during April causing mortality to increase by thirty per week at its peak. The spatial impact of this high mortality reflected the existing pattern in the distribution of poverty across the union. Despite the increased mortality caused by the cholera epidemic in Mullingar this area had a lower death rate in 1849 than in 1847.[112] This implies that the higher overall mortality for 1849 was caused by increased famine-related deaths in the poorer western districts. The excess mortality in this union thus mirrored the existing general distribution of poverty here. The 1848 failure also affected the rate of recovery from famine conditions in areas like Ballynacarrigy because it adversely influenced the acreage planted with potatoes in 1849.

The answer to the question as to why mortality peaked in this union in 1849 must start with the potato failure of 1848. However, it is more legitimate to ask why mortality wasn't much higher. The crop failure of 1848 was as extensive in this region as that of 1846. However the government's relief measures, in particular the soup kitchen act, were much more effective in 1847 than was the total reliance on the poor law in 1849. One quarter of the population of the union received soup rations in 1847 compared to the 3.5 per cent relieved in the workhouse in 1849. One reason for the lower relative mortality in 1849 was undoubtedly the lower food prices resulting from the cheap grain imports.[113] It is also reasonable to assume that many of the labourers, cottiers and small farmers had emigrated and were thus spared the consequences of the 1848 failure.[114] The new rail connection between Mullingar and Dublin facilitated this exodus from the union. The addition of third and fourth-class carriages to this service in early 1849 indicates increased demand from the poorer classes as the renewed distress forced them to join the thousands now leaving the country.[115] Significantly these new fares were one way only the return ticket being available only, to first and second class passengers.[116]

The efficient administration of the union by the vice guardians may also account for the relatively low mortality rates in Mullingar union in 1849. This was evident in their effective response to the cholera epidemic.[117] There were many pleas to the commissioners to allow them to continue in office, particularly as it was envisaged replacing them in the middle of arguably the worst crisis in the union since the partial failure of 1845. Many of these pleas came from landlords who did not relish the task of administering to the wants of the 2,545 paupers then resident in the parent house and its auxiliaries. The fact that they had to take over the administration of the union as it faced into the hungry season made this prospect all the more uninviting.[118] The commissioners' decision to replace Ward and Dillon with elected guardians in the middle of this crisis, is indicative of their preference for bureaucratic procedures now that the union's finances were in order.[119] The new board of guardians continued the policies initiated by the vice guardians and they were if anything now more rigorous in their interpretation of the poor law. Their task was made somewhat easier by a gradual easing in famine conditions for the poorest classes during the summer of 1849. This was indicated by the general reduction in the poor rate levied in 1849. The rail connection between Mullingar and Athlone, which would pass through some of the poorest districts in the union, started in June.[120] G.A. Boyd, the deputy chairman of the Midland Great Western railway and a poor law guardian in this union, secured employment for able-bodied paupers on this project. One thousand inmates left the poor house during the summer and by the end of August all the able-bodied paupers had left it.[121] The potato harvest of 1849 was generally blight free and the price of this staple food started to return to its pre-Famine level. The easing of the crisis was indicated by the closure of the Dublin Bridge, Rathconnell and Irishtown auxiliaries.[122] There was a general realisation that the union had passed through the 'ordeal of providence' which had left no class 'unscathed'.[123] The demise of the Westmeath Farming Society during the summer of 1849 indicated the effects of the repeated failures on the local farm economy. The landlords had financed the society and the tenant farmers were the main competitors for its prizes. Tuite defended the discontinuance of his financial contribution to the society and his resignation from the board of guardians by stating that he now had to concentrate on repaying his debts. Great hopes had been invested in the society when it was founded some ten years previously. Lord Westmeath offered £100 to help build an agricultural hall in Mullingar. The society's annual ball in Murray's hotel was the social highlight for this mainly agricultural community. Landlords and tenants could meet on neutral ground to promote their common interests when the society met during the year. Its collapse was equally symbolic. The unity of the agricultural community, which the society's founders hoped it would achieve, was destroyed by the Famine. Each section of this community had 'been scathed in some degree' by the 'visitation of providence'.

Consequences

'... they are emigrating here from all nations, day after day, night after night, week after week to such a degree that I should not wonder if this country would become as bad as the old one'.[1]

When Matthew Gaynor wrote to his parents in Knockdrin during the spring of 1849 he asked them to thank a neighbour, Mick Lovely, for 'telling him to go to America' following the first potato failure of 1846. The son of a comfortable tenant farmer on the estate of Sir Richard Levinge, he was now working as a carpenter in Utica and he asked his parents to send out details of the many young men from the 'mountain parish' who had emigrated in the intervening two years. He was so happy with his new life in America that he said he would advise them all to come over 'only there would be nobody left to mind the old women'. He realised that some 'great change' had happened in Knockdrin when a well off neighbour called James North, had decided to emigrate. He concluded by inquiring as to how 'the poor were getting through life' after the latest potato failure. The 21 per cent decline in the population of the reconstituted Mullingar poor law union[2] between 1841 and 1851 was the most obvious immediate effect of the economic crisis this area was still going through when the census enumerators published their returns in 1852.[3]

The most significant demographic declines occurred in the poor western small farm zone, between Glenlough and Castletown (fig. 9). The biggest losses here occurred in the south-western districts of Castletown and Killare where 53 and 40 per cent of their respective populations either died or emigrated between 1841 and 1851. These areas had the highest pre-Famine population densities and were the poorest districts in the union. Subdivision, non-residence and a high dependence on potatoes meant that this area was extremely vulnerable to the successive harvest failures. The labourers inability to pay the conacre rents combined with the very high rates levied in this region, meant that the exodus was not confined to the less well off class. The smaller ratepayers were severely affected by the sustained harvest failures and the collapse in agricultural prices in 1848. The one-third decline in the number of farms between fifteen and thirty acres was as high as the reduction in the number of labourer's plots under one acre and indicates the general impact of the crisis on all those farming under thirty acres in this union.[4]

A second broad zone of more moderate demographic decline occurred along the north eastern and southern margins of the union. These com-

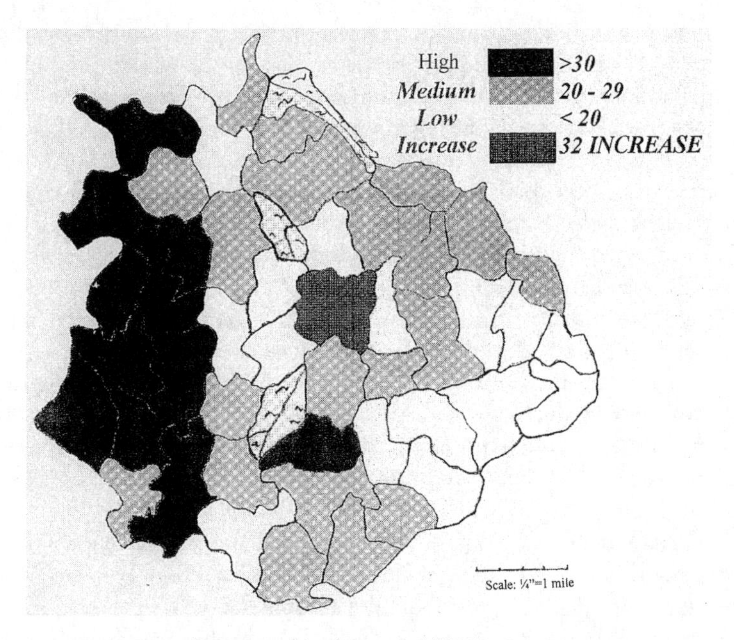

9. Demographic change in MPLU 1841–1851

paratively richer areas had moderate population densities before the Famine. This was reflected in their lower relative population declines immediately after it. However, heavier losses occurred in districts like Kilbixy, Middleton, Newtown and Portloman, all of which were contiguous to the poorer western districts. The fear that the destitution prevalent in these latter areas would engulf their areas may partly explain the flight of almost one third of these areas population. The comparatively higher pre-Famine population densities of these north-eastern districts also meant that a sizeable proportion of this now 'redundant' population had decided to leave.

The eastern districts, through which the newly laid Midland Great Western railway passed, had smaller population declines despite having moderate to high pre-Famine population densities. The work provided for the labouring population on this project, particularly in 1848 when food prices were falling, may explain the lower levels of population loss in these areas. The central lakes region had the fewest post Famine adjustments to make at least in so far as this can be measured by demographic decline. The best land in the union was found in this area and the prevalence of grazier farms resulted in lower population densities. The moderate demographic impact of the Famine on these central and eastern districts was indicative of successful earlier adjustments to changing economic circumstances. Landlord residence was high in this region which in turn reflected the wealth of the area as well as its easy access to the capital. The 32 per cent increase in the population of Mullingar was due to the almost 1,500 paupers still resident in the workhouse and its auxiliary in Linen street.[5] The influx of labourers to the town's cabin suburb of Cabbage street from the distressed western districts, seeking work on the Mullingar-Athlone railway, accounts for the rest of the increase.[6] The decline in Carrick shows more affinity with the impoverished western districts than with the 'broad acres' of the grazier zone in which it was located. The many evictions carried out in this area in 1849 indicate the effects of the accumulated stresses here following the 1848 failure.[7] These evictions in turn were indicative of the mounting pressures on landlords as some of them were forced to dispose of their estates in this area immediately after the Famine.[8] Carrick constituted the northern part of Clonfad in the original territorial template of the poor law administrators. As such it was one of the areas which was badly affected by the partial failure of 1845. Its consequent distress was brought regularly to the authority's attention by the local Protestant rector, Rev. William Eames.[9]

Emigration did not account for the entire population decline in the union. Excess mortality caused by the Famine resulted in the deaths of between 1,329 and 1,747 people.[10] This excess mortality accounted for 14.5 per cent of the population loss between 1845 and 1851. The two major killer diseases associated with the Famine were dysentery and fever.[11] Dysentery or 'the bloody flux' as it was popularly known, was directly attributable to the change in the peoples diet especially the consumption of raw turnips and maize.[12] There were several deaths from dysentery in Moyvore in February 1847 because the people were forced to live 'chiefly on turnips' and 'loaf bread' before the public works restarted.[13] This disease, which was often referred to as 'bowel complaints' was prevalent in Killare, Kilbride, Collinstown, Newtown, Portnashangan, and Taughmon.[14] Indeed such was the fear of dysentery that the soup kitchen in Knockdrin was closed because of the perceived link between soup and dysentery.[15] There were two types of fever during the famine – relapsing fever or yellow fever and the dreaded typhus or black fever.[16] Both were infectious and were spread by the common body louse *pediculus humanus*, which proliferated during the famine as beggars and the evicted crowded the food depots, the relief works and the workhouse.[17] Fever had accompanied the failure of 1845 in Ballymore where entire families were 'smitten'.[18] However the prevalence of the disease following the failure of 1846 necessitated the opening of a temporary fever hospital in Mullingar market house in February 1847.[19] These Famine related diseases and the higher mortality experienced in this union in 1847 were inextricably linked.

In Mullingar parish, mortality peaked in 1847 exceeding births for the first and only time during the Famine (fig. 10).[20] This figure represented an increase of 150 per cent on what may be described as the base year of 1844 thus suggesting that 'black '47' was the year of greatest distress in the Mullingar area.

There is also a significant correlation between the prices demanded for potatoes in Mullingar in 1847 and mortality in the town (fig. 11). April was the month of highest mortality and it was also significantly the month of highest potato prices.[21] The fact that there were no potatoes for sale during the previous three months and that the price of meal had reached Famine levels, also contributed to this high mortality. The saw toothed seasonality pattern displayed for both potato and oat prices broadly reflects the convulsions experienced in this union between 1845 and 1849. This was particularly the case in 1847, when the price of potatoes and oats was 500 and 255 per cent higher respectively in May of that year, than during the corresponding month in 1845. The crisis also impacted on the number of marriages and births. One measure of the severity of the crisis in Mullingar is the fact that only twenty-nine marriages took place in the Catholic church in the town in 1847. This represents a fall of 50 per cent in the mean marriage rate between 1844 and 1849.[22] This fall in the marriage rate undoubtedly affected the decline in the number of births but this may also have been caused by amenorrhoea.[23] Under nourishment and malnutrition leads to a cessation of menstruation. Thus, there is a direct link between the acute distress experienced here in 1847 and the decline in fertility. Others may of course have suppressed the luxury function of reproduction in order to preserve the vital function of survival. The increase in mortality in Mullingar in 1847 was replicated in the rural districts of the union.[24]

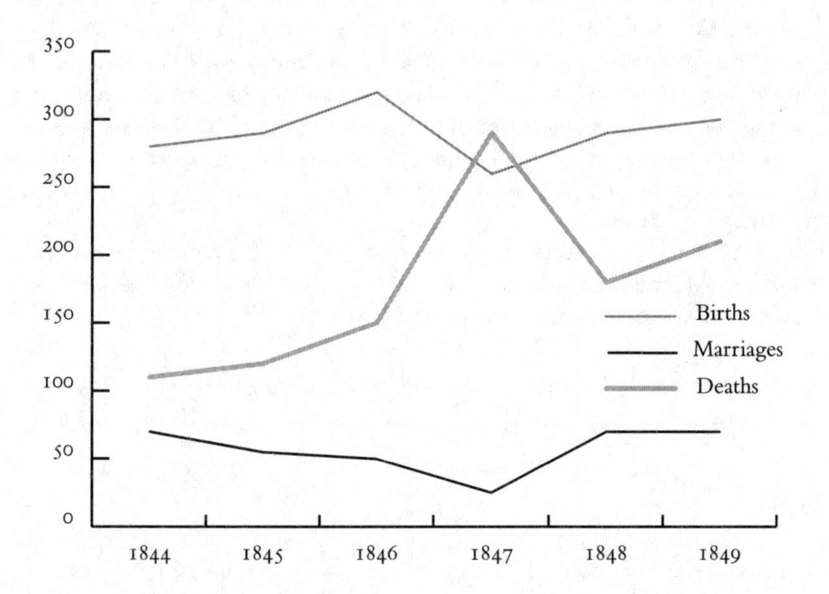

10. Births deaths and marriages in Mullingar parish 1844–9

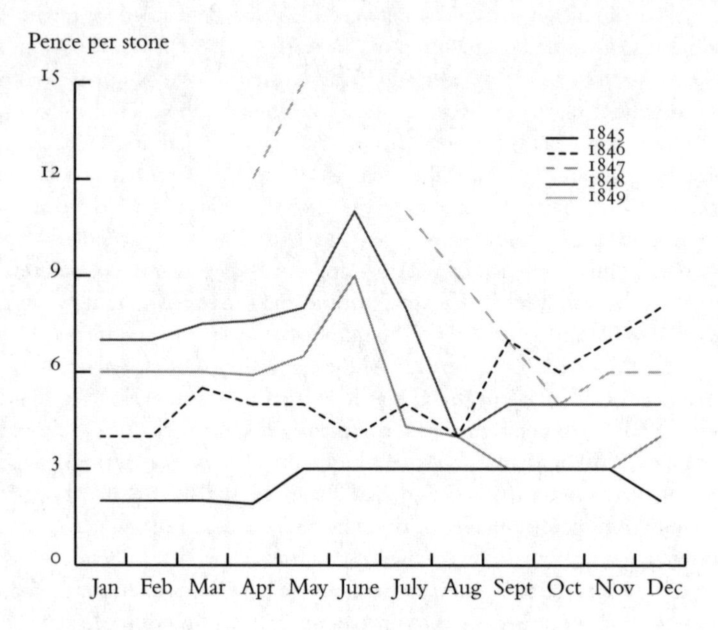

11. Price of potatoes in Mullingar 1845–9

The spatial distribution of these Famine deaths reflected the overall pattern of outward migration. However it was much more socially selective as the labourers and cottiers bore the brunt of Famine mortality.[25] The variegated territorial pattern depicted in this analysis of demographic decline reveals the complexity of the micro regional impact of the great Famine. The socio-economic consequences were equally complex and in many ways they replicate and support the conclusions reached in the examination of the areal impact of the potato failures.

The combined effects of the successive failures and poor prices for agricultural produce were all too obvious by 1849.[26] Farm output declined in all the major agricultural enterprises (table 1).[27]

Table 1 Number of sheep on agricultural holdings in MPLU 1847–49

	Less than one acre	1–5 acres	5–15 acres	15–30 acres	Over 30 acres
1847	523	300	2042	4893	53112
1849	123	127	1031	2591	42733
% decline	76%	57%	49%	47%	19%

Table 2 Structural changes in farm size in MPLU 1847–49

	Less than one acre	1–5 acres	5–15 acres	15–30 acres	Over 30 acres
1847	1550	1432	1802	1887	2016
1849	1033	1047	1491	1258	1948
% decline	33%	26.8%	17.2%	33%	3.3%

Sheep and cattle rearing dominated the local economy and their decline was indicative of the economic cost of the Famine to this mainly pastoral region. The 23.4 per cent decline in sheep numbers between 1847 and 1849 was caused by the slaughter of these animals on open pastures by the starving labourers, as well as the inability of the small farmers in particular, to replenish their stocks. The 39 per cent fall in potato acreage in 1849 was indicative of the renewed loss of confidence in this staple food and delayed recovery in the poorest areas from the immediate consequences of the Famine. Purdue's comment that 'no class had escaped unscathed' was true as far as overall agricultural production was concerned. However the crisis had a disproportionately adverse effect on those farming less than thirty acres (table 2).[28]

One third of the cottiers farming between one and five acres had become day labourers. Another third of the labourers having less than an acre in 1847 were landless three years later. Equally significant however was the one-third decline in holdings between fifteen and thirty acres. This comfortable class of farmer had suffered the combined effects of the loss of con acre rents and a loss of farm income caused by their need to consume farm produce following the potato failures.[29] The additional expense of high poor rates especially in the western small farm zone convinced many of these 'substantial farmers' that their best interests were served by emigrating.[30] Equally important was their ability to pay the expensive fare to either north or south America. As they arrived daily 'by the hundred' in Dublin immediately after the 1848 failure, it was observed that 'all were well provided' for the Atlantic crossing. This class had also observed the impoverishment of the groups immediately beneath them in the social hierarchy and their superior education and knowledge of opportunities elsewhere, especially Argentina, enabled them to react quickly to avoid what they perceived as their pending impoverishment.[31] The loss of this able class, especially in the poorer districts, was one of the longer-term deleterious consequences of the Famine. The relatively lower decline in the number of those whose holdings were between five and fifteen acres may reflect their lower exposure to poor rates or the lack of the financial resources necessary for the transatlantic crossing. Taken together, the holdings of these two groups of small farmers had declined by a quarter in the three years following the 1846 failure. This contrasted with the insignificant 3 per cent fall in the number of holdings over thirty acres. In fact the grazier class had consolidated its position during the Famine and was relatively unaffected by it. The percentage of farms in this union with acreages exceeding thirty acres increased from 23 to 28.7 per cent while all the other categories declined. This group also enhanced its existing dominance of the union's pastoral economy. 91 per cent of the union's sheep and 75 per cent of its cattle were now reared on the grazier's pastures. Their economic dominance resulted from this group's ability to benefit from the change to pastoral husbandry before the Famine. It was enhanced during the Famine at the expense of all those farming less than thirty acres but especially those immediately below them in the social hierarchy. Even though landlords formed the wealthiest segment of the grazier class, they were more exposed to the adverse effects of the Famine than their more substantial tenants. They suffered a decline in rental income, especially where their estates were located in the poorer districts.

Landlords also had to pay higher poor rates than the tenants because they were liable for the rates of those whose property was under £4 valuation. Some estates, like the Lanesboro property near Rochfortbridge and the Malone estate in Killare were encumbered with debt before the Famine. The additional losses incurred during the Famine meant that many of these now bankrupted estates were sold. The Encumbered Estates Act facilitated the sale of these heavily mortgaged properties. Most auctions took place in the western districts where the existing poor economic structures were worsened by the potato failures.[32] Almost one third of the townlands in the barony of Moycashel were sold between 1847 and 1855.[33] Castletown and Streamstown, two of the poorest and most densely populated districts in the union were in this barony. Landlords in the Rathconrath area were also adversely affected by the failures as 22 per cent of this barony's townlands acquired new owners during the early 1850s. Landlords in the central lake district escaped relatively unscathed as very few auctions took place in this area. However one notable property changed hands right in the heart of this prosperous zone. The town of Mullingar, which formed the most valuable portion of the Granard estate, was purchased by Col Fulke Greville for £120,000.[34] His marriage to the marquis of Westmeath's only surviving child ensured continuity in the midst of the precipitous changes that were now affecting this area.

John Charles Lyons was elected chairman of the re-appointed board of guardians of this union in April 1849. His Ledeston estate was located two miles south of the town on the picturesque eastern shores of Lough Ennel or Belvedere Lake, as the gentry preferred to call it. Lyons was a keen gardener and he kept up a regular correspondence with his friend Sir William Hooker, who was curator of Kew gardens near London. However there was little reference to plants in his correspondence to Hooker in December 1849.[35] His letter was one long complaint about the effects of the Famine on his rental income. His tenants were 'behind with their rents' but he was afraid to evict them because he feared the consequences of being denounced as an 'exterminator'. Many of these farmers were reneging on their debts and selling their cattle and their crops to finance their departure to the new world.[36] One of the most unusual destinations for migrants from Ireland at this time was chosen by thousands of people from this union.[37] Argentina was over 7,000 miles and almost one month's-sailing time from Mullingar.[38] The fact that emigrants were advised to bring a revolver as well as a saddle may not have deterred farmers who had been forced to protect their flocks from starving labourers. Argentina would soon become the most important sheep rearing country in the world and this partly explains its attractions to the farmers of this union especially the small farmers whose sheep stocks had declined by 75 per cent during the Famine. The pattern of migration from south Westmeath to Argentina was established by a successful businessman called Pat Bookey from Streamstown. He went there in 1830 and his success encouraged others to seek their fortune there in the 1830s and 1840s. A Fr Fahy from Loughrea was also a very important contact for the new arrivals.[39] Dr Cantwell's correspondence with him is indicative of the strengthening links between the two areas during the 1840s.[40] These links intensified during the Famine and continued until the 1880s.

The majority of migrants from Ireland to Argentina came from Westmeath with smaller proportions from Longford and Wexford. The importance of the established pre-Famine pattern of migration from this area became obvious during and immediately after the Famine as movement out of a small ten-mile zone focused around Ballymore intensified. This pattern reflected the fortuitous coincidence of this area's pre-Famine migratory contact with 'rich' Argentina. Emigrants remittances probably enabled some of the poorer classes leave these areas to work in the Argentinean saladeros or as shepherds on the Pampas. Overall however only small to medium sized farmers could have afforded fares which ranged from £10 for a steerage passage to £35 for first class passengers. This socially selective nature of the movement to Argentina is obvious from Bishop Cantwell's recommendation to Fr Fahy of a Cunningham family from Ballymore. He told Fahy that this family belonged to 'that valuable class the emigration of which must ere long prove the ruin of Ireland'.[41] The economic ruin that the Famine threatened on this class is implicit in this family's decision to leave immediately after the second major failure of the potato crop in 1848, despite the fact that one of its members was mid way through his studies for the priesthood. Thomas Cunningham was sixty-two when he left Ballymore with his wife, his five daughters and two sons. Having sold his stock and possessions and purchased the sailing tickets from Mulvihill's general grocery store in nearby Ballymahon,[42] the family made its way to Dublin from the then terminus of the Midland Great Western railway at the Hill of Down. From there they sailed to Southampton where they boarded the ship which would take them to Buenos Aires. The passage to the river Plate estuary was 'as smooth as a mill pond' apart from the inevitable storms they encountered in the Bay of Biscay. As the ship sailed up the Tagus to pick up more passengers in Lisbon, they could admire the 'delightful Cintra, the old castle of Belem' or the city port crowded with war vessels and merchant shipping. If they ventured ashore they could marvel at the 'six storied stone buildings' which Pombal designed to replace those destroyed by an earthquake almost one hundred years previously. Their last coaling station before the south Atlantic crossing was at San Vincente.[43] The only sign of life on this barren rock was some lemon trees in pots near the customs house. Ten days later they sailed up the river Plate estuary to start their new life over 7,000 miles from the scene of 'this present awful calamity' and a poor law system still struggling with the aftershocks of several successive harvest failures.[44] One son hoped to continue his studies for the priesthood. The other son, Thomas junior, fulfilled the dream of all the migrants from Westmeath at this time of becoming 'as rich as an Argentinean'.

The author William Bulfin was the editor and proprietor of the Irish paper in Argentina – *The Southern Cross*. His wife was from Ballymore and when he toured this area on his bicycle some fifty fears after the Famine, the landscape he described was quite different to that familiar to his wife's family during the Famine.[45] More than one half of the population had emigrated mostly to Argentina. Gone also were most the fourth class hovels of the labourers and cottiers.[46] The broad pastures of the graziers stretched to the horizon in every direction. As he passed by the 'Royal' hill of Uisneach he failed to notice the most recent layer on the historical landscape of this area.[47] The ruins of the Famine village on top of Carn hill and the now fossilised lazy beds which supported it, were already part of local Famine folklore.[48] However, his happiest encounter as he passed through 'the turf belt' occurred in Moyvoughly. When the turf cutters heard that he had come from Argentina they stopped their work and gathered round him as he told stories of the Pampas 'to the brothers, sisters, nieces and nephews' of people he had met there. His happy description of the excitement of his listeners suggests that the Famine was not a totally unmitigated disaster for this area and is certainly a welcome antidote to the distress, dysentery and desolation their friends neighbours and relations faced fifty years previously.

Conclusion

One of the most striking features of the economy of this union, on the eve of the Famine, was its duality. Alongside the increasingly dominant and commercialised grazier holdings there coexisted a subsistence small farm economy and its dependent labourers that was still recovering from the latest of the cyclical crises that afflicted it each decade. For the poorest labourers in this 'mud cabin and fat bullock' economy, hunger and distress were their habitual cabin mates each 'starving summer'.

The government's response to the partial failure of 1845 was effective in this union. Food prices were controlled through the distribution of Indian corn and employment on public works was provided in the poorer districts. Consequently, the twelve months which followed the partial failure of 1845 would be more accurately characterised as a subsistence crisis than as an outright Famine. The total failure of 1846 brought widespread Famine conditions to the poorest areas and classes in the union. The failure of the potato crop was aggravated by the government's policy of insisting that the relief committees sell the oaten, wheaten and Indian meal alternatives at local Famine prices. The reliance on public works throughout the winter and spring of 1846–7 helped relieve the distress of the able bodied labourers. However the high levels of excess mortality experienced by both old and infirm people, and young children in this union is indicative of the shortcomings of this policy. The success of the subsequent soup kitchen act is evidenced by falling mortality here immediately after its introduction. The incremental impoverishment of the cottiers and those farming up to ten acres was a feature of the Famine experience here following the failure of the potato in 1846. The failure of 1846 also revealed the spatial duality of the union's economy as a very distressed western zone emerged in contradistinction to a relatively unaffected south-eastern corridor contiguous to the recently commenced Midland Great Western railway works. However, high pre-Famine population densities, subdivision and absenteeism rendered the western small farm zone extremely vulnerable to the cumulative potato failures in this area. Those who either sought to escape from this poverty and distress through emigration, or succumbed to it through disease or death came from those whose holdings were under ten acres or were landless labourers.

The government's declaration that the Famine was officially over in this and other unions in 1847 indicated their determination to make the poor law unions totally responsible for all the distress in their areas. The conjunction of this abrogation of responsibility and the second total failure of the potato crop in this union in 1848, meant that 1849 was the worst year of the Famine in this union. The increased mortality was borne by the less well off classes but this time the vice guardians' decision to discontinue outdoor relief resulted in a notable increase in mortality among the able-bodied labourers. These labourers were the unwitting victims of the presumption that the unions undoubted relative wealth was evenly distributed. However, distress following the 1848 failure was not confined to those whose holdings were less than ten acres. The Gregory quarter acre clause, the collapse in livestock and grain prices, the substantially increased poor rates as well as the potato failure destabilised all those whose holdings were under thirty acres. Because of their relative prosperity in comparison to the landless labourers, these small holders lost most during the Famine. The prospect of sharing the annual starving summers with their landless neighbours must have been a truly traumatic experience for them. The absolute distress suffered by the labourers and their families is evidenced by the high excess mortality rates experienced in this union in 1847 and 1849. This class was also forced to eventually submit to the workhouse test in large numbers. The government's decision to channel all relief through a poor law system dependant on local rates meant that the labourers had either to submit to the 'repugnant test' or emigrate. The one-fifth reduction in the population of this union during the Famine indicates that most who could afford to took the latter option. They did not adopt these seemingly inevitable options passively however. Like all the other social groups in this union, they endeavoured to protect themselves from the consequences of the potato failures. The grazier's 'turnip minding houses' and their acquisition of substantial quantities of arms in 1846 suggests the threat the less well off classes posed to the 'respectable portion' of the community throughout the union. Implicit in Tuites refusal to countenance large numbers of labourers congregating in quarries in 1848 was his acknowledgement of their disaffection and his fear that this could be harnessed onto the political ideals of the Young Irelanders. The small farmers use of violence against process servers, landlords, land grabbers and rate collectors is indicative of the similarity in the responses of these two groups to a crisis which threatened their livelihoods in this union.

In contrast to all those farming under thirty acres the grazier class was relatively unaffected by the Famine in this union. This was implicit in the landlord's decision to exclude those farming over thirty acres from the rent abatements, which followed the two major failures. Their position was also strengthened because of their lower relative exposure to poor rates. Their increased confidence expressed itself almost immediately after the Famine in demands for tenant right. This posed yet another threat to the increasingly precarious position of the landlords. They had faced considerable criticism during the Famine particularly those who were absentees or who had evicted tenants following the potato failures. Their non-residence in parts of the poorer districts of this union augmented the distress experienced by the labourers and cottiers of these areas. Many of the communities of interest in the union viewed the landlords as the class most likely to help them through the crisis. Labourers sought employment from them. Small tenant farmers sought rent abatements following the potato failures. The graziers shared a common interest with the landlords in ensuring that the workhouse test was rigidly enforced after 1847. However, their domination of the union's political and economic structures was severely tested during the Famine. The challenge to their hegemony crystallised around the able and determined leadership provided by Bishop John Cantwell. His curates in Mullingar represented the increasing confidence with which the emergent Catholic middle class partook in the relief committees, the board of guardians, political agitation against evicting landlords and the government's relief policies. His involvement in the tenant right movement after the Famine helped the cause of the class, which would replace the landlords just fifty years later.

Finally it is necessary to answer the question posed in the introduction – how bad was the Famine in this area? Historians have divided the country into four zones, which experienced varying levels of distress during the Famine.[1] The north and the west represent the extremes with relatively little in the former and extreme distress in the latter. The rest of the country falls into two halves – the eastern with less than a fifth of its population indigent for at least a year between 1846 and 1850, and a western where the proportion of paupers remained at more than a fifth and less than a half throughout the crisis. Mullingar poor law union occupies this latter area and thus its Famine experience lies somewhere between the devastation it caused in the west and its characterisation as a subsistence crisis in the east. This categorisation is useful for contextualising the effects of the potato failures on this union. However, the value of micro-regional analyses of the Famine emerges from this study. The extremes experienced nationally were also found in this relatively small area. This bipolarity is the most notable feature of the Famine in this union. Demographic change ranged from the loss of 53 per cent of Castletown's population during the Famine to Mulingar's 32 per cent increase during the same period. Dependency on soup rations exceeded the national average in some of the western districts while the Lynn area south of Mullingar was self-sufficient. The poorest labourers in every district lived on Lumper potatoes while the grazier's herds got a house, potato land, grass for their cows and between £10 and £15 per annum. The union's median geographical location between east and west was reflected in its microcosmic replication of the Ireland's Famine experience. This east west spatial dichotomy mirrored the complex social implications of the Famine for the union's various communities of interest. It is only within these social and spatial parameters that the impact of the Great Famine on Mullingar poor law union can be fully understood and contextualised.

Notes

ABBREVIATIONS

H.C.	House of Commons
CSORP	Chief Secretary's Office Registered Papers
N.A.	National Archives
N.L.I.	National Library of Ireland
R.I.A.	Royal Irish Academy
W.G.	*Westmeath Guardian*
F.J.	*Freeman's Journal*
O.P.W.H.	Outrage Papers Westmeath
M.D.A.M.	Meath Diocesan Archive Mullingar
P.R.O.	Public Record Office, London
W.C.L.	Westmeath County Library
M.P.L.U.	Mullingar Poor Law Union

INTRODUCTION

1 Cormac Ó Gráda, *Ireland before and after the famine. Explorations in economic history, 1800–1925* (Manchester, 1993), p. 98.
2 Cecil Woodham Smith, *The Great Hunger*, (London, 1981).
3 E. Estyn Evans, *The personality of Ireland, habitat, heritage and history* (Dublin, 1992), p. 18
4 Raymond Gillespie, Myrtle Hill (eds) *Doing Irish local history, pursuit and practice* (Belfast, 1998), pp 1–21.
5 Brian Ó Dálaigh, Denis A. Cronin, Paul Connell, (eds), *Irish townlands*, (Dublin, 1998), p. 9.

MULLINGAR POOR LAW UNION BEFORE THE FAMINE

1 Wriothesley Noel, 'Notes on a short tour through the Midland counties of Ireland in the summer of 1836' in Jeremiah Sheehan: *Westmeath as others saw it* (Moate, 1982), p. 100.
2 *The parliamentary gazetteer of Ireland 1844–45* (3 vols, Edinburgh, 1846), ii, p. 828.
3 J.H. Andrews, A. Simms, H.B. Clarke (eds), *Irish historic town atlas, no. 5, Mullingar* (Dublin, 1992), p. 4.
4 *W.G.*, 7 May 1840.
5 *Bill for the more effective relief of destitute poor in Ireland [as amended in committee, and on recommitment]*, H.C., 1837–38, (238), v, p. 345.
6 *Appendix to minutes of evidence before select committee on colonisation from Ireland*, H.C., 1847, (737)(737–11) vi, p. 176.
7 Christine Kinealy, Trevor Parkhill (eds), *The Famine in Ulster* (Belfast, 1997); Ignatius Murphy, *A people starved-life and death in west Clare* (Dublin, 1996).
8 Samuel Lewis, *A topographical dictionary of Ireland* (2 vols., London, 1837), ii, p. 696.
9 Virginia Crossman, *Local government in Ireland in the 19th century* (Belfast, 1994), p. 15.
10 Michael Kenny, 'The structure of agriculture in east Westmeath 1820–1846', unpublished MA thesis U.C.D. 1974; *Select committee on colonisation from Ireland*, H.C, 1847, (737), (737–11), vi, p. 307.
11 *Evidence taken before Her Majesty's Commission of inquiry into the state of law and practise in respect of the occupation of land in Ireland*, H.C., 1845, (672), xxxiv; hereafter *Devon Commission*; evidence of Richard Reynell p. 311, and Anthony Sutton p. 321.
12 N.A., Tottenham Papers; A list of tenants removed from the estates of Sir Francis Hopkins at Rochfort, 1836–43.
13 Alexander Somerville, *Whistler at the plough* (Manchester, 1852), p. 513.
14 *Devon Commission*, evidence of Richard Reynell, p. 314.
15 *Devon Commission*, evidence of Thomas Glennon, p. 315.
16 E.T. Mulhall, *Handbook of the river Plate* (Edinburgh, 1885), p. 109; *Devon Commission*, evidence of Thomas Glennon, p. 314.
17 *Devon Commission*, evidence of David Harton, p. 323.
18 Wriothesley Noel, *Notes of a tour through the midland counties of Ireland, in the summer of 1836* (London, 1837), p. 100.
19 Edward Wakefield, *An account of Ireland, statistical and political* (London, 1812), p. 626.
20 *Census of Ireland 1841* H.C., [504], xxiv, p. 116.
21 *Devon Commission*, evidence of Anthony Sutton. p. 321.
22 *First report of His Majesty's Commission for inquiring into the conditions of the poorer classes in Ireland*, H.C., 1835, (369), xxxii, Appendix D, hereafter *Poor Law Inquiry*.
23 *Poor Law Inquiry*, Supplement to Appendix D. Evidence of Rev. Augustus Potter, Rathconrath, p. 187.
24 *Devon Commission*, Evidence of Anthony Sutton p. 321.
25 *Poor Law Inquiry*, Supplement to Appendix D; evidence of Rev. John Reed, Enniscoffey, p. 181.
26 *Devon commission*, evidence of William Fetherston Haugh, p. 310. *W.G.*, 16 June 1842.
27 *Poor Law Inquiry*, Supplement to Appendix D; evidence of Gerald Dease, p. 129.
28 Margaret Crawford, (ed.), 'William Wilde's table of Irish famines, 900–1850' in E. Margaret Crawford (ed.) Famine the Irish experience 900–1900 (Edinburgh, 1989), pp 18–22.
29 Austin Bourke, *The visitation of God? The potato and the Great Irish Famine* (Dublin, 1993), p. 42.
30 Smith, *Great Hunger*, p. 28.
31 *Devon Commission*, evidence of William Fetherston Haugh p. 310.
32 N.A., RLFC4; Austin Bourke, 'The extent of the potato in Ireland at the time of the famine', in *Farming since the famine* (Dublin, 1997), p. 389.
33 *Poor Law Inquiry*, evidence of Rev. John Reed, p. 181.

34 *Poor Law Inquiry*, evidence of Rev. Meade Dennis, Lynn p. 189.
35 *Poor Law Inquiry*, evidence of Rev. John Falloon, Ballymore, p. 192.
36 *W.G.*, 25 Sept. 1845.
37 *The parliamentary gazetteer of Ireland 1844–45*, ii, p. 516.
38 N.A., MS. 5990.
39 *Devon Commission*, evidence of William Fetherston Haugh, p. 309.

THE ALL ABSORBING QUESTION OF THE POTATO DISEASE, 1845–6

1 N.A., R.L.F.C/1 1474; John Ball A.P.L.C. describing conditions in Killare.
2 Christine Kinealy, *This Great Calamity, the Irish Famine 1845–52* (Dublin, 1994), p. 32.
3 *W.G.*, 30 Oct. 1845.
4 N.A., RLFC2/Z14512; 14818; 16494.
5 N.A., RLFC2/ Z14818
6 N.A., RLFC2/ Z16342.
7 N.A., RLFC2/ Z 852.
8 *W.G.*, 27 Nov. 1845.
9 N.A., RLFC2/ Z 16342.
10 N.A., RLFC2/ Z 16082.
11 *Poor Law Inquiry*, Supplement to appendix D, evidence of Rev. Eames, p. 124.
12 N.A., RLFC2/ Z 852.
13 N.A., RLFC2/ Z 852.
14 Smith, *Great Hunger*, p. 40.
15 Smith, *Great Hunger*, p. 40.
16 N.A., RLFC2/ Z 15012.
17 Kinealy, *This Great Calamity*, p. 35
18 *Copy of report of Dr. Playfair and Mr. Lindley on the present state of the potato crop and the prospect of approaching scarcity, 15th Nov. 1845*, H.C., 1846, xxxvii, p. 28.
19 N.A., RLFC4.
20 N.A., RLFC4.
21 N.A., RLFC3/1 917.
22 Smith, *Great Hunger*, p. 48.
23 Kinealy, *This Great Calamity*, p. 38
24 N.A., RLFC3/1/1048.
25 N.A., RLFC3/1/1343; *W. G.*, 24 Apr. 1846.
26 N.A., RLFC2/ Z 14296.
27 *W.G.*, 19 Nov. 1845.
28 N.A., RLFC2/ Z 16342.
29 N.A., Tottenham papers. A list of tenants removed from the estates of Sir Francis Hopkins at Rochfort, 1836–1843.
30 *F.J.*, 27 Jan. 1846.
31 N.A., C.R.F. 1 S 1846.
32 N.A., O. P.W.H. 1846: 30/1813.
33 N.A., RLFC1 Abstracts 7/3/46–16/3/46.
34 Smith, *Great Hunger*, p. 35; the loss was also much greater than previous estimates-see Mary Daly *The Famine in Ireland* (Dundalk, 1986), p. 54, where Westmeath's loss was placed at between 0 and 19 per cent.
35 N.A., RLFC3/1 917.
36 U.C.D., School's Folklore Collection S196 p. 132.
37 N.A., RLFC1 Abstracts 7/346–17/3/46.
38 N.A., RLFC3/1 915; 1004.
39 *W.G.*, 16 Nov.1845.
40 *W.G.*, 16 Nov. 1845.
41 N.A., RLFC3/1 1535.
42 N.A., RLFC2/ Z 852.
43 N.A., RLFC1 Administrative, 12 Dec. 1845.
44 Smith, *Great Hunger*, p. 76.
45 N.A., RLFC2/Z 852; RLFC1 Administrative, 7–17 Mar.1846; RLFC/1/325.
46 N.A., RLFC3/1 /1474.
47 N.A., RLFC3/1/1535.
48 N.A., RLFC3/1/787,317.
49 N.A., RLFC3/1/325.
50 N.A., RLFC3/1/1474; *Returns of medical officers and fever hospitals, gaols and dispensaries*, H.C., 1846, xxxvii, p. 120.
51 N.A., RLFC/1/1474.
52 Kinealy, *This Great Calamity*, p. 38.
53 *Census of Ireland 1841*, H.C., [504], xxiv, p. 151.
54 N.A., RLFC/2 Z 852.
55 N.A., RLFC/1 Z 852; N.L.I., Ms. 11700 Designs for agricultural buildings suited to Irish estates.
56 N.A., RLFC/1/1535.
57 N.A., LEC Rentals, vol. 8, no. 21; RLFC3/1/5160.
58 N.A., RLFC2/ Z 852.
59 Jeremiah Sheehan, *Worthies of Westmeath*, (Moate, 1987), p. 88.
60 N.A., RLFC3/1/931, 3520.
61 N.A., C.R.F. IS, 1846.
62 N.A., RLFC3/1/1535.
63 N.A., RLFC3/1/1596.
64 N.A., RLFC/1/708.
65 N.A., RLFC/1/931.
66 N.A., RLFC/1/5160.
67 Smith, *Great Hunger*, p. 78.
68 N.A., O. P.W.H. 1846: 30/73730.
69 *W.G.*, 11 Jun. 1846.
70 N.A., O. P.W.H., 1846: 30/7676.
71 N.A., O.P.W.H. 1846:30/6715.
72 N.A., RLFC4.
73 *W.G.*, 26 Mar.1846.
74 *W.G.*, 3 June 1847.
75 N.A., RLFC 3/1/708, 781, 904, 1514, 1535.
76 *W.G.*, 26 Mar. 1846.
77 *F.J.*, 9 Jan.1846.
78 Smith, *Great Hunger*, p. 86.
79 Kinealy, *This Great Calamity*, p. 86.
80 N.A., RLFC3/1/5591.
81 N.A., RLFC3/1/3326.
82 *W.G.*, 2 July, 1846.
83 *W.G.*, 30 July 1846.
84 N.A., RLFC3/1/326.

THE SAD DIMINUTION OF FOOD, 1846–7

1 R.I.A., Ms., 24 Q 28, f.497.
2 *W.G.*, 13 July, 1846.
3 *W.G.*, 13 Aug., 1846.
4 N.A., RLFC5 30/02.
5 N.A., RLFC5 30/ 04.
6 N.A., RLFC5 30/ 07.
7 N.A., RLFC4.
8 N.A., RLFC5 30/02.
9 N.A., RLFC7 30/25.
10 Kinealy, *This Great Calamity*, p. 71.
11 9 & 10.Vic. cap. 107.
12 *Times*, 26 Sept. 1846.
13 *W.G.*, 8 Oct. 1846.
14 N.A., RLFC3/2/30/44.
15 N.A., RLFC7/30/04.
16 N.A., RLFC3/3/30/09–44.
17 N.A., RLFC/3/30/09; 29.
18 N.A., RLFC/3/2/30/32.
19 *W.G.*, 25 Mar 1847; N.A., RLFC 3/2/30/28.
20 N.A., RLFC3/2/30/28.
21 N.A., RLFC/3/2/30/28.
22 N.A., RLFC7/30/12.
23 N.A., C.S.O.R.P., D 5264.
24 Alfred P. Smyth, *Faith, Famine and Fatherland* (Dublin, 1992), p. 61.
25 *Correspondence relating to the measures adopted for the relief of distress in Ireland*, (Board of Works series), *second part*, H.C., 1847, (797), lii, p. 115.
26 N.A., RLFC3/2/30/32.
27 N.A., RLFC7/30/31.
28 R.I.A., Ms., 24 Q 28, f.460; N.A., RLFC/3/2/30/19.
29 N.A., RLFC/3/2/30/06.
30 N.A., RLFC7/30/31.
31 N.A., RLFC3/2/30/38.
32 N.A., RLFC3/2/30/38.
33 R.I.A., Ms., 24 Q 27, f. 239; *W.G.*, 27 Aug. 1846.
34 N.A., CSORP, O.P.W.H., 1846, 30/28117.
35 *W.G.*, 29 Oct. 1845; W.G., 7 Jan 1846; *W.G.*, 28 Feb.1846; *W.G.*, 18 Mar.1846; *W.G.*,11 Apr.1846; *W.G.*, 15 May 1846.
36 N.A., CRF 7m, 1843; CRF N15, 1847; Convict Reference Book 3 (1844–1850).
37 N.A., C.S.O.R.P.,O. P.W.H. 1847 30/265.
38 N.A. TR6–11, Transportation Registers, 1845–1851.
39 N.A., Prisons 1/9/7; register of female convicts Grangegorman Depot 11 July 1840–22 Dec. 1853.
40 *W.G.*, 10 June, 1847.
41 N.A., C.R.F., 20W, 1847.
42 *W.G.*, 31 Dec. 1846; N.A.I. RLFC7/10; *Correspondence relating to the measures adopted for the relief of distress in Ireland* (Board of Works Series), *first part*, H.C., 1847, l, p. 393.
43 Rev. William Clare (ed.), *A young Irishman's diary being extracts from the early journal of John Keegan of Moate* (New York 1928), p. 97, hereafter Keegan, *A young Irishman's diary*.
44 N.A., C.S.O.R.P., O.P.W.H., 1847.30/114.
45 N.L.I., Ms. 5990.
46 N.A., RLFC7/30/31.
47 R.I.A., Ms. 24 Q 28, f. 497.
48 N.A., RLFC7/30/25.
49 R.I.A., Ms. 24 Q 28, f. 497.
50 N.A., C.S.O.R.P., D 1322.
51 *W.G.*, 26 Nov. 1846.
52 R.I.A., Ms. 24 Q 27, f. 170.
53 N.A., RLFC7/30/24.
54 R.I.A., Ms. 24 Q 27, f. 169.
55 N.A., RLFC7/30/25.
56 *W.G.*, 28 Jan. 1847.
57 N.A., RLFC 730/25.

58 R.I.A., Ms. 24 Q 28, f.169.
59 R.I.A., Ms. 24 Q 28, f. 169.
60 R.I.A., Ms. 24 Q 28, f. 434; N.A., RLFC/3/2/30/31.
61 N.A., RLFC/3/2/30/35; R.I.A., Ms. 24 Q 28, f. 470.
62 N.A., RLFC7/30/05.
63 *W.G.*, 5 Nov. 1846.
64 *W.G.*, 5 Nov. 1845.
65 R.I.A., Ms. 24 Q 28, f.169.
66 N.A., RLFC7/30/37.
67 N.L.I., Wilson's Hospital Rental Ms. 3098; Boyd Rental Ms. 3108.
68 N.L.I., Ms. 7909.
69 W.G.,1 July, 1847.
70 *Returns from the courts of queens bench*, H.C. 1849 (315), xlix, 235, pp 4–6.
71 *Evicted destitute poor (Irl.) Act. Return to an order of the honourable H.O.C. 19th Feb. 1849 for return of notices served upon relieving officers of poor law unions entitled an act for the protection and relief of the destitute poor evicted from their dwellings.* 11&12 Vict. C. 47, p. 27.
72 U.C.D., Folklore Commission, S196, p. 332.
73 *W.G.*, 8 Apr. 1847; N.A., C.S.O.R.P., O.P.W.H., 1847, 30/78.
74 *W.G.*, 31 Dec. 1846.
75 *W.G.*, 7 Jan. 1847.
76 *W.G.*, 10 Nov. 1846.
77 *W.G.*, 8 Apr. 1847.
78 R.I.A., Ms. 24 Q 28, f. 460; N.A., RLFC3/2/30/10.
79 N.A., RLFC3/2/30/32; R.I.A., Ms. 24 Q 27, f. 169.
80 R.I.A., Ms. 24 Q 27, f. 239;as the only people of standing in the local community were 'petty shopkeepers', the Rev. Battersby asked the Board of Works inspector to sign the requisition to the relief organisation.
81 N.A., RLFC3/2/30/29.
82 *W.G.*, 20 May, 1847.
83 N.A.,RLFC3/2/30 29
84 *Papers relating to proceedings for the relief of distress . . . in Ireland*, H.C., 1849, [1042], xlviii, p. 118.
85 *Correspondence relating to the measures adopted for the relief of distress second part*, p. 115.
86 N.A., RLFC3/2/30/42.
87 9 & 10 Vic. cap.107.
88 N.A., RLFC3/2/30/33.
89 *W.G.*, 24 Sept. 1846.
90 *Correspondence relating to the measures adopted for the relief of distress first part*, pp 213, 367.
91 *Correspondence relating to the measures adopted for the relief of distress, first part*, p. 376.
92 R.I.A., Ms.24 Q 28, f. 373; *Correspondence relating to the measures adopted for the relief of distress, first part*, p. 209.
93 N.A., RLFC7/12.
94 *W.G.*, 24 Dec. 1846.
95 Keegan, *A young Irishman's diary*, p. 97.
96 Keegan, *A young Irishman's diary*, p. 104.
97 N.A., RLFC7/30/ 12.
98 *Correspondence relating to the measures adopted for the relief of distress, first part*, p. 254.
99 N.A., RLFC7/30/25.
100 N.A., RLFC7/30/17.
101 Kinealy, *This Great Calamity*, p. 99.
102 *W.G.*, 10 Dec. 1846.
103 *Correspondence relating to the measures adopted for the relief of distress, first part*, p. 414.
104 *Correspondence relating to the measures adopted for the relief of distress, first part*, pp 119, 126, 446.
105 N.A., RLFC3/2/30/11.
106 N.A., RLFC7/30/20.
107 Personal communication from Sir John Nugent Oct. 1997.
108 N.A., RLFC3/2/30/23.
109 R.I.A., Ms. 24 Q 27, f. 203.
110 N.A., RLFC7/30/12.
111 *Correspondence relating to the measures adopted for the relief of distress, second part*, p. 208.
112 *W.G.*, 24 Dec. 1846.
113 Kinealy, *This Great Calamity*, p. 99.
114 M. D. A. M. Register of births, marriages and deaths, 1843–51.
115 N.A., C.S.O.R.P., O.P.W.H., 1847: 3–0/99.
116 *Correspondence relating to the measures adopted for the relief of distress, first part*, p. 318.
117 N.A., C.S.O.R.P., O.P.W.H., 1847:30/201.30/99.
118 N.A., C.S.O.R.P., O.P.W.H., 30/199.
119 N.A., C.S.O.R.P., O.P.W.H., 30/201.
120 N.A., RLFC3/2/30/38.35.
121 Mary E. Daly, *The Famine in Ireland* (Dundalk,1986), p. 87;10 Vic. Cap. 7.
122 N.A., C.S.O.R.P., O. P.W.H. 1847:30/201;30/99;30/199; C.S.O.R.P. Distress papers, D1227; D1847.
123 *F.J.*, 17 Feb. 1847.
124 N.A., RLFC 7/30/17.
125 R.I.A. I., Ms. 24 Q 27; 24 Q28; 24 Q29; 24 Q30; N.L.I., MS 5372.
126 Keegan, *A young Irishman's diary*, p. 97.
127 R.I.A. I., Ms. 24 Q 27,ff. 162, 203, 208, 239; 24 Q 28, f.460; 24 Q 29, ff. 651, 1048, 1127, 1162; N.A., RLFC 3/2/30/10; 21; 32; 35.
128 *W.G.*, 25 Mar. 1847; R.I.A. Ms. 24 Q 27, f. 208
129 R.I.A., Ms. 24 Q 28, f.239.
130 N.A., C.S.O.R.P., Distress Papers, D5264, 1847.
131 Daly, *The Irish Famine*, p. 88.
132 *Supplementary appendix to the seventh report from the Relief Commission*, H.C., 1847–1848, [956], xxvii, p. 70.
133 *W.G.*, 24 June 1847.
134 N.A., RLFC7/30/25.
135 *Report of the commissioners appointed to take the census of Ireland for the year 1841*, H.C., 1843, xxiv, pp 120, 121.
136 T.W. Freeman, *Pre-famine Ireland* (Manchester, 1960), p. 93.
137 *Supplementary appendix to the seventh report from the Relief Commission*, H.C., 1847–1848, [956], xxvii, p. 70.
138 Daly, *The Irish Famine*, pp 88–89; Cormac Ó Gráda, *The Great Irish Famine* (Dublin, 1995), p. 45; James S. Donnelly, Jr. 'The soup kitchens', in W.E. Vaughan (ed.), *A New History of Ireland, v, Ireland under the union 1: 1801–1870* (Oxford, 1989), pp 307–315.
139 Kinealy. *This Great Calamity*, p. 133.

THE INDIVIDUALISATION OF RESPONSIBILITY 1847–9

1 N.A., C.S.O.R.P., O 7019.
2 *W.G.*, 8 July, 1847.
3 *Returns of agricultural produce in Ireland in the year 1847*, part I, Crops, [923], H.C., 1847/48, lvii, p. 100.
4 N.A., RLFC4.
5 Austin Bourke, 'The extent of the potato crop in Ireland at the time of the famine', in *Farming since the famine* (Dublin, 1997), p. 382.
6 Kinealy, *This Great Calamity*, p. 179.
7 *W.G.*, 16 Sept. 1847.
8 *Papers relating to proceedings for the relief of distress and the state of the unions in Ireland; sixth series*, H.C., 1848,[955], lvi, pp 973–1000; hereafter *Telford report*, p. 993.
9 *W.G.*, 14 Oct. 1847; *W.G.*, 28 Oct. 1847.
10 *W.G.*, 16 Dec. 1847.
11 *W.G.*, 25 Jan. 1848; Poor Law Extension Act 10 Vic. C. 56. 10&11 Vic. c. 84.90.
12 *W.G.*, 9 Dec. 1848
13 *W.G.*, 10 Feb. 1848.
14 *W.G.*, 23 Dec. 1847
15 *Statistical abstracts for each poor law union 1848–49*. H.C., 1849, [1096] [1117], xlvii, 766, 783, p. 998.
16 *Telford report*, pp 973, 974, 978, 980, 988, 988, 992, 998.
17 *W.G.*, 8 May 1848.
18 *Telford report*, pp 975, 980.
19 *W.G.*, 9 Jan. 1849.
20 N.L.I., Rental of the estate of G. A. Boyd, 1839–54, Ms. 3108.
21 *Telford report*, p. 979.
22 *W.G.*, 25 Jan. 1849.
23 Kinealy, *This Great Calamity*, p. 180.
24 *Devon Commission*; evidence of Thomas Glennon, p. 314.
25 *W.G.*, 6 Apr. 1848.
26 *Telford report*, pp 973, 974, 980, 984, 991, 993.
27 *W.G.*, 20 Jan 1848; Tuite wanted the guardians to allow the paupers till these plots rather than have them congregating in quarries breaking stones.
28 *Telford report*, p. 980.
29 *Papers relating to proceedings for the relief of distress and state of the unions*, p. 15.

30 Kinealy, *This Great Calamity*, p. 218; many of those entering the workhouse in 1848–49 were deserted wives and their children, (*W.G.*, 3 May 1849).
31 N.A., C.S.O.R.P. O 1609, O 2407.
32 *Devon commission*, evidence of Richard Reynell. p. 314.
33 *W.G.*, 5 Oct. 1848; *W.G.* 25 Jan. 1849; the graziers could now send their cattle directly to the Smithfield market thus eliminating the local 'salesmasters'.
34 Kenny, 'The structure of agriculture in east Westmeath 1820–1846', p. 74
35 *Telford report*, pp 974, 977, 988, 993, 999.
36 *W.G.*,20 Jan. 1848.
37 *Telford report*, pp 980–982.
38 *W.G.*, 27 July 1848.
39 *Telford report*, p. 993.
40 Kinealy, *This Great Calamity*, p. 177.
41 *Telford report*, p. 993.
42 *W.G.*, 11 May 1848; Tuite's comment that the guardians would look 'odious' in the eyes of the people if they implemented the 'starvation policies' of the commissioners is indicative of this fear.
43 *Inspectors report on distress of unions in reply to circular of inquiry to poor law inspectors as to state of crops.* H.C., 1848, lvi, p. 14
44 *W.G.*, 13 Jan.1848; *W.G.*, 5 Oct. 1848.
45 *Telford report*, p. 997.
46 *Telford report*, p. 998.
47 *W.G.*,18 May, 1848.
48 *Telford report*, p. 973.
49 *W.G.*, 10 May, 1848.
50 *W.G.*, 15 June, 1848.
51 *W.G.*, 6 July, 1848.
52 *Statistical abstracts for each poor law union 1848–1849.* H.C., 1849, [1096] [1117], xlvii, p. 998.
53 *Papers relating to proceedings for the relief of distress and the state of the unions and workhouses in Ireland.* H.C., 1849,[1042], xlviii, p. 56.
54 *W.G.*, 3 Aug. 1848.
55 *W.G.*, 5 Oct. 1848.
56 S.H. Cousens, 'The regional variation in mortality rates during the Great Irish Famine', in *Proceedings of the Royal Irish Academy*, lxxi, C (1963), p. 141.
57 *W.G.*, 25 Jan. 1848.
58 *W.G.*, 5 Oct. 1848.
59 *W.G.*, 12 Apr. 1849.
60 *Papers relating to proceedings for the relief of distress and the state of unions and workhouses in Ireland.* H.C., 1849, [1042], xviii, p. 56.
61 *W.G.*, 5 Oct. 1848.
62 *W.G.*, 5 Oct. 1848.
63 *W.G.*, Jan 25 1849.
64 *Papers relating to proceedings for the relief of distress and the state of the unions and workhouses in Ireland*, H.C., 1849, [1042], xliviii, p. 115.
65 *Papers relating to proceedings for the relief of distress and fate of the unions and workhouses in Ireland*, p. 115.
66 *W.G.*, 25 Jan. 1849; see comments of speakers on emigration of farmers to America.
67 *W.G.*, 28 Dec. 1848; *W.G.*, 25 Jan. 1849; Tuite paid a rate of 5*s*.11*d*. and Robinson 5*s*. 8*d*.; these were similar to rates levied in the West and both landlords complained about the burden they had to bear.
68 *W.G.*, 25 Jan 1849; landlord contributions to the court house debate are indicative of their disenchantment with the administration of the poor law.
69 *W.G.*,18 Jan. 1849.
70 *W.G.*, 25 Jan. 1849.
71 N.L.I., Wilson's Hospital Rental Ms.3098; Boyd Rental, Ms. 3108; Trinity College Library. Incorporated Society, schools and estates rental, Ms.5501–02.
72 *W.G.*,25 Jan. 1849.
73 *W.G.*, 20 Sept.1849; one of the criticisms of the vice guardians was their decision to source some of the union house's needs outside this region; *W.G.*, 22 Mar. 1849.
74 *W.G.*, 20 Sept.1849.
75 *Return of the valuation of each electoral division in Ireland with its population in 1841 and the total poundage directed to be raised by any rate or rates made upon every such electoral division during the year ending*, 31st Dec. 1847, H.C., 1847/48, (311), lviii, p. 10; similar returns for 1848 /49, H.C. xl, p. 12, li, p. 12.
76 Kinealy, *This Great Calamity*, p. 246; S.H. Cousens, 'The regional variation in mortality rates during the Great Irish Famine', p. 139.
77 *W.G.*, 10 May, 1849.
78 *W.G.*, 31 May, 1849.
79 *W.G.*, 1 June, 1848.
80 *W.G.*, 7 Dec. 1848.
81 *W.G.*, 11 Oct. 1848; 7 Nov. 1849.
82 *W.G.*, 31 May 1849; the young female paupers were housed in the basement portion of the Irishtown auxiliary which previously functioned as a barn. The boys occupied the more habitable upper storeys.
83 *W.G.*, 21 June, 1849.
84 *W.G.*, 30 Nov. 1848.
85 *W.G.*, 6 Sept 1848; *W.G.*, 19 Apr. 1849.
86 *W.G.*, 31 May, 1849.
87 *W.G.*, 5 July, 1849
88 *W.G.*, 31 May, 1849.
89 *W.G.*, 16 Feb. 1849.
90 *Irish Historic Town Atlas, no. 5, Mullingar*, p. 40.
91 *W.G.*, 7 Dec. 1848.
92 *W.G.*,30 Aug. 1849
93 *W.G.*, 1 Feb. 1849.
94 *29th report of the Inspector General on the state of prisons of Ireland 1850 with appendices*, H.C., 1851, xxviii, p. 51.
95 *W.G.*, 6 Sept. 1849.
96 *W.G.*, 7 Dec. 1848
97 *W.G.*, 14 Dec. 1848.
98 *W.G.*, 28 Dec. 1848.
99 Dympna Mc Loughlin, 'Superfluous and unwanted deadwood. The emigration of nineteenth century Irish women', in Patrick O Sullivan (ed.) *The Irish world-wide*, (Leicester, 1997) p. 67; *W.G.*, 1 Feb. 1849.
100 *W.G.*, 10 May 1849.
101 S.H. Cousens, 'The regional variation in mortality rates during the Great Irish Famine', p. 141.
102 *Census of Ireland for the year 1851; Table of deaths in workhouses and auxiliary workhouses and workhouse hospitals; number of deaths by localities and causes*, H.C., 1852–53, ii, pp 84–85.
103 S.H. Cousens, 'The regional variation in mortality rates during the Great Irish Famine', pp 141–143.
104 *W.G.*, 31 May, 1849.
105 *W.G.*, 26 May 1849.
106 *W.G.*, 17 Mar.1849.
107 N.A., C.S.O.R.P., O.P.W.H., 1849. O7019.
108 *W.G.*, 10 May, 1849.
109 *W.G.*, 28 Jan. 1849; 9 Oct. 1849.
110 *W.G.*, 3 May, 1849.
111 *W.G.*, 19 Apr. 1849.
112 M.D.A.M., register of births, deaths and marriages 1844–1849.
113 Irish College, Rome Archives, Cullen Papers, no. 1694.
114 *W.G.*, 25 Jan. 1849; many speakers commented on the 'farmers' emigrating to America.
115 S.H. Cousens, 'The regional pattern of emigration during the great Irish Famine' in *Population studies*, xiv, no. 1 (July 1960) p. 133. P.R.O., Letters of John Charles Lyons, Vol. 28, no. 1846.
116 *W.G.*, 1 Mar. 1849.
117 *W.G.*, 19 Apr. 1849.
118 *W.G.*, 22 Mar. 1849; James Fetherston Haugh from Bracklyn, wondered how 'gentlemen and farmers' could look after the needs of 2,000.
119 Kinealy, *This Great Calamity*, p. 216.
120 *W.G.*, 28 June, 1849
121 *W.G.*, 30 Aug. 1849.
122 *W.G.*, 6 Sept. 1849.
123 *W.G.*, 22 June, 1849.

CONSEQUENCES

1 N.L.I., Ms. 13554, Letters from Matthew Gaynor to his parents in Clonkill.
2 *Return showing the arrangements made by the commissioners for administering the laws for the relief of the poor in Ireland* . . . H.C. 1851, (447), xliv, pp 465–469, a new workhouse was built in Delvin in 1852 on land acquired from the marquis of Westmeath; the Mullingar union was reduced in size by 10 per cent and by 11,000 in population.

3 *Comparative view of the census of Ireland 1841–1851*. H.C., 1852, (373), xlvi, p. 32; based on a projected population growth of 5 per cent between 1841 and 1851; there was a 7 per cent growth in population here during the previous decade.
4 *Returns of agricultural produce in Ireland for the year 1847; Stock*, H.C., 1847–48, [1000], lvii, pp 90–91; *Returns of agricultural produce* . . . 1849, [1245]; H.C., 1850, li, 39, pp 162–163.
5 *W.G.*, Jan.–Dec. 1851.
6 *W.G.*, 25 Jan. 1849.
7 *W.G.*,5 July, 1849.
8 Andreas Eiriksson, Cormac Ó Gráda, *Estate records of the Irish Famine. A second guide to famine archives, 1840–45* (Dublin, 1995), p. 62; N.A., LEC vol. 2, no. 7.
9 N.A., RLFC3/1 787,904,1514.
10 Joel Moykr, *Why Ireland starved. A quantitative and analytical history of the Irish economy 1800–1850* (London, 1993), p. 267; based on a projected population of 66,482 and Moykr's estimate of between 20 and 26.3 excess deaths per 1000 of the population in this region.
11 R. Dudley Edwards, T. Desmond Williams (eds), *The great Famine* (Dublin, 1994), pp 265–270.
12 Smith, *The great hunger*, p. 187.
13 R.I.A., Ms. 24 Q 28, f. 497.
14 R.I.A., Ms. 24 Q 28, ff. 169, 208; 24 Q 29, ff. 651, 662, 980, 1044, 1048.
15 R.I.A., Ms. 24 Q 29, f. 1048.
16 Smith, *Great hunger*, pp 49–50.
17 Lawrence M. Geary, 'The late disastrous epidemic', in Chris Morash, Richard Hayes (eds) *Fearful Realities-new perspectives on the famine* (Dublin, 1996), p. 50.
18 R.I.A., Ms. 24 Q 27, f. 169.
19 *W.G.*,13 May, 1847.
20 M.D.A.M. Register of births, deaths and marriages, 1843–1851.
21 *W.G.* 1845–49; Ó Gráda, *Ireland before and after the famine.* p. 144.
22 M.D.A.M. Register of births, marriages and deaths, 1844–49.
23 E. Le Roy Ladurie, 'Amenorrhoea in time of famine' in *The territory of the historian* (Chicago, 1979), p. 263.
24 N.L.I., Pos. 4168; Representative Church Body Library, Dublin, registry book of Delvin p. 2/36/1.1; R.I.A., Ms. 24 Q 29, f. 662.
25 *W.G.*, 5 Apr. 1849; Bryan Sheerin's 'extremely emaciated' body was found in a field in Lynn shortly after he had spent the day working with the local rector the Rev. Dennis; John Nugent's body was found at the side of the road in Skeagh, Rathconrath; he died from a 'rupture of an intestine caused by previous destitution' (*W.G.*, 29 June 1848); N.A., C.S.O.R.P., O 8227; death of Anne Keenahan, a labourer from Streamstown, during the summer of 1849 due to destitution.
26 P.R.O., Letters of John Charles Lyons, vol. 28, no. 1846.
27 *Returns of agricultural produce in Ireland for the year 1849*, stock, H.C., 1850, li, p. 58.
28 *Returns of agricultural produce in Ireland 1849*, [1245], H.C., 1850, li, pp 162–166.
29 R.I.A., Ms. 24 Q 27, f. 169.
30 Smith, *The Great Hunger*, p. 368.
31 Euardo Coghlan, *Los Irlandes en la Argentina. Su Actuacion Y decennaencia* (Buenos Aires, 1987), p. 207.
32 N.A., LEC, vol. 8, no. 21.
33 Andreas Eriksson, Cormac Ó Gráda, *Estate records of the Irish Famine*, p. 62.
34 W.C.L. The sale of Mullingar from Lord Granard to Lord Greville 1856, Philip Tierney, *Mullingar in old picture postcards* (Zaltbommell, 1995), p. 57.
35 P.R.O., Letters of John Charles Lyons, vol. 28, no. 1846.
36 David Fitzpatrick, 'Flight from famine', in Cathal Poirtéir (ed.), *The Great Irish Famine*, p. 176 (Dublin, 1995).
37 Eduardo A. Coghlan, *Los Irlandes en la Argentina. Su Actuacion Y decennaecia.*
38 E.T. Mulhall, *Handbook of the river Plate* (Edinburgh, 1885), p. 109.
39 Thomas Murray, *The story of the Irish in Argentina*, (New York, 1919) p. 56.
40 Eduardo *Coghlan, Los Irelandes en la Argentina. Su actuacion Y decennaecia*, p. 207.
41 Eduardo Coghlan, *Los Irelandes en la Argentina. Su actuacion Y decennaecia*, p. 207.
42 Dick Stokes, Sean Finn, 'Emigration and population trends', in Jeremiah Sheehan (ed.) *Beneath the shadow of Uisneach* (Mullingar, 1996),p.192.
43 E.T. Mulhall, *Handbook of the river Plate*, p. 110.
44 *Times*, 26 Sept. 1846; workhouse numbers remained in the mid 1,500s throughout 1850 and 1851 thus showing the long drawn out nature of the famine experience for the poorer classes in the union. *W.G.*, 1850–51.
45 William Bulfin, *Rambles in Eirinn* (Dublin, n.d.) p. 414.
46 *Census of Ireland 1911. General report with tables and appendices*, p. 348; just 1 per cent of the union houses were in the 4th class category in 1911 compared to almost 40 per cent in 1841.
47 U.C.D., Folklore Commission, S. 196 p. 353; evidence of Mairead Mac Manus, Loughnavalley.
48 U.C.D., IFC 1075: 464–474. Evidence of Mick Kelly, Gartley, Castletown-Geoghegan; his father was born in 1830 and survived the Famine.

CONCLUSION

1 S. H. Cousens, 'The regional pattern of migration during the Great Irish Famine 1846–1851' in *Population Studies*, xiv, no. 1 (1960), p. 123.